IT IS TIME

A memoir of reconciliation embracing various spiritual traditions, healing the Armenian Genocide and the Feminine Wound, and claiming the call of a Divine Mother

TINA KARAGULIAN

Black Rose Arts & Press
San Antonio

Black Rose Arts & Press
P.O. Box 6707
San Antonio, TX 78209
www.tinakaragulian.com

Cover, book design and logo by Tina Karagulian.
Photograph on back cover by Marcy Maloy.
Reprinted with permission. www.marcymaloy.com

Immaculée Ilibagiza, *Left to Tell: Discovering God Amidst the Rwandan Holocaust,* (with Steve Erwin), (Carlsbad, CA: Hay House, Inc.), Copyright ©2006. Permission granted by the publisher. For a complete list of copyright permissions, see the *Permissions* section at the end of this book.

Karagulian, Tina, 1965–
    It Is Time: a memoir of reconciliation embracing various spiritual traditions, healing the Armenian Genocide and the Feminine Wound, and claiming the call of a Divine Mother / Tina Karagulian

ISBN: 978–0983804208

1. Women—Spirituality. 2. Memoir 3. Women—Psychology. 4. Self-perception. 5. Poetry.

Printed in the United States of America on recycled paper.

This book is dedicated to all the women and men who have walked with the Divine, and those who are in the process of remembering.

The greater the darkness, the greater the light.[1]

Kay Briggs

Longer Now

Walk the trees,
The inside out,
The limbs that fall,
While singing the years
You might have wanted & dreamed.
Walk them now,
The longer trees,
The longer streams;
Flourish in the mash of reverential hoopla,
Of God's Good Grace.
The Black Rose Lighthouse beckons:
Your dreams,
Your songs,
Your stories—
All yours to claim.[2]

For the TinaHouse: paschal booker

Table of Contents

Longer Now	1
Acknowledgements	5
Preface	9
She	11
Descent	12
Divine Mother	15
Surrender	16
I Will Praise God, My Beloved	25
Heart Opening	26
Longing	34
Spiritual Awakenings	36
Der Eem Asdvadz	41, 42
Prayers	42
See-faring	45
Ocean Rebirth	46
You Preserve Me	51
Role as Caretaker	52
The Right of Your Passage	59
Deepening Prayer: Releasing Outcome	60
Jagadakeer	65
My Grandmother and the Armenian Genocide	66
Stories from Zeitun	70
The Return	78
Community	82
Memories of Halep	86
Little Girl Vision	92
Crossroads	94
Adolescence	96
Still-born	101
Should I Stay or Should I Go?	104
It Does Not Matter	109
Side by Side	110
Body Memories	126
A Touch	134
Whatever It Takes to Heal	136
Dream of Pomegranates	144
The Annunciation of My Soul	149

Motherhood: Birthing Voice and Child   150
New Skin   154
Ask and You Will Receive   156
Walden   160
My Heart is Full   167
Reconciliation   168
Bending Into   171
Mid-life: Coming Full Circle   172
Mother's Day Sermon   178
Teaching a Child to Dance   184
Genocide and the Feminine Wound   186
Outrage   202
Truth and Forgiveness   212
Holy Conversations   218
Reconciliation—the Circle Widens   224
All Matter of Communion   230
Divine Feminine   232
It Is Time   238
Epilogue   241
Appendix A: Renunciation Sermon   243
Appendix B: Mother's Day Sermon   249
Bibliography and Notes   259
Permissions   277

Acknowledgements

I am thankful to my Creator, whose many names grace these pages. She has mothered me with wisdom and nurturing, fulfilling every need from my soul. She and Christ have been constant in their love and guidance throughout my life, and without their assistance, I could not have written this book. Many times when I felt the task was daunting, I felt them gently guiding my focus.

I acknowledge that my many blind spots will not be fully reflected in this book, and I ask forgiveness for those omissions. I am confident that in the years to come, I will receive more insight, wisdom, growth, and compassion.

I thank my grandmother Zarman (Meguerditchian) Megherian for choosing to tell her stories to her daughter, and my mother, Siran (Megherian) Karagulian, for telling me the same stories each time I asked. Their love and their longing for a better life for their children and grandchildren were the impetus for this book.

I am so grateful for my husband Paschal (Pat) Booker, for *making my soul shine*. I thank him for his attention to detail, as he edited each sentence of this book; his suggestions and clarifications have been invaluable, and I am forever indebted to him. Pat and our son Walden Booker support me on so many levels with their perspective and their abiding love. They have brought me back to life more than once, and they constantly show me how easy living in joy and love can be. This book is for my future grandchildren, that they may know that my love for them is infinite: it is but one testament of that love.

I thank these beautiful people as well: My father Louis Karagulian and my uncle Noubar Karagulian (Unk), for loving me with incredible tenderness, proving that love can overcome a painful childhood, and that art and music are ways to recover what was lost. Rev. Fr. Vartan Megherian (Kerry) and his wife Yeretzkin Yefkin Megherian, who took in and tended many Armenians who journeyed to America and established Armenian Church communities there. Their leadership also made a difference for many members of our family. Lisa (Karagulian) Carroll, Ardis Karagulian, Lena Megherian, Talin Megherian—my sisters and cousins—are dear to my heart. My husband's parents, Gretel and Tom Ekbaum, who tended to a portion of our lives when we needed it. I send blessings to the women and men of the Megherian, Karagulian, and Ekbaum clans.

The poetry and friendship of Diana Der-Hovanessian have been beacons to me in more ways than I can ever put into words. Diana kept the poetic fire burning bright within me for the day when I would bring it forth.

Thank you, Terry Arata-Maiers, Rosalyn Collier, Christina Guerra, Lilas Harvey, Barbara Maloy, and D. Phelps for your keen editing eyes and for how you lovingly read my stories and held them in prayer—your hands, heart, and wisdom helped midwife this book into the world.

Many other spiritual sisters and brothers have helped me to discern moments when I needed to hear my own process. They shared their wisdom with me, modeling how to shine my light in the world, and how to balance speaking truth with loving tenderness: Maria Alejandro, Terry Arata-Maiers, Zet Baer, Ona Banks Barnes, Milo Beaver, Kay Briggs, Angela Brittain, Melanie Christenson, Melinda (Hess) Cooke, Priscilla Coppock, Saradell Crawford, Erma Crumedy, Rev. Fr. Mikael Devejian, Dru Dunn, Mary C. Earle, Rosalyn Falcon Collier, Susan Damon, Olga Samples Davis, Zimmie and Ara Eloian, David Ferguson, Perla Garcia, Michelli Gomez, Xelena González, Marilyn Graham and Sheila Korte, Mary Ellen Galloway, Susan (Sam) Gilliam, Martha K. Grant, Christina Guerra, Deborah Hanus, Betty Hart, Lilas Harvey, Onaskha Hernandez, Judy Hess, Isabelle Hindin, Alice Holden, Dal Hucknall, Deborah Hurst, Susan Ives, Eleanor Johnson, Paula Jurigian, Rev. Arnak Kasparian, Trudy Kenyon, Lucy Kimatian, Gina Lalli, Maureen Leach, Bertha Luna, Ruth Lindahl Brown, Sylvia Maddox, Lisa Mason, Barbara Maloy, Rose Marden, Marise Melson, Shakti Miller, Carol Monroe, Archbishop Tiran Nersoyan, Arpine and Haig Panoyan, Jane Patterson, Donna Peacock, D. Phelps, Narjis Pierre, Carla Pineda, Dee Pye, Ralph Ransom, Jodi

Roberts, Otilia Sánchez, Patsy and Edwin Sasek, Jack Sheffield, Joseph Smith, Jean Springer, Gwendolyn Stallings, Jeanette Sullivan, Bill and Stewart Swann, Carol Sydney, Louise Taylor, Virginia Tourigian, Aminah Ulmer, Yahaira Volpe, Robert Walden, Rachel Wester, and Sona Yeghiayan.

I thank the many members of church communities that have welcomed me and my family, embraced my gifts, and who have taught me that love can transcend any limitation; especially, members of St. Sahag and St. Mesrob Armenian Apostolic Church and The Episcopal Church of Reconciliation. The Reconciliation choir has been a tight-knit family, showing me that when our unique voices can come together as one voice, it is not just a dream, but a real vision for our world. I want to thank Alan Arata-Maiers for encouraging me to write my first sermon, Rev. Robert Woody, who has given me a place to share many sermons, and all those who have encouraged my voice through poetry, writing, teaching, and singing.

To Diana Der-Hovanessian, Rosalyn Falcon Collier, Paula D'Arcy, Sherry Ruth Anderson, Margaret Ajemian Ahnert, Carol Edgarian, Sue Monk Kidd, and Clarissa Pinkola Estés: thank you for sharing your heart and soul through your writing and through your stories. Your contributions gave me permission to speak from my vulnerable places, and to shine love through them.

There are so many more who have encouraged me through their books, their stories, and their holy conversations. I thank you all.

Preface

I am a story gatherer. Some collect marbles, baseball cards, charms, or special stones. I collect stories of the heart. Some of the stories I have collected from loved ones became so much a part of me that it was difficult to know where they ended and I began.

The time is ripe for the stories to leave my body and take form. They must be voiced, brought into consciousness, and given a new perspective, in order to shift the course for future generations. That is my goal.

My hope is that these stories may bring healing to all who lived the stories and to those who bore witness to them. Each time I have expanded my perspective, my cultural concept of community has also expanded. As I remember all the people who have touched my life, even those who do not share my family or ethnicity, I claim them all as my true community. They have given me pearls of their wisdom, encouragement, and their loving hearts, so that I might heal. From that broadened perspective, I can look back upon my life and know that I have never been alone. Through my inner and outer journeys, a divine spark has always been present to guide me.

That spark has helped me to sift through the stories I have carried in my belly. I have walked the journey of my Armenian grandmothers, and I have carried the burden of suffering for others. Sometimes I took on too much, sometimes not enough, and sometimes I held others in a centered place, so that their own abilities to balance might awaken. Finding that centered, balanced space—learning how to be present to another's suffering while holding my own center—is my life's work. Bringing these stories to form, giving them voice, has been integral to that centering process.

I have watched women bear stories in their wombs. Some women become mute because the stories are too painful to tell, yet they pass along the unspoken words nonetheless; some women intentionally tell their stories to their daughters and sons, so that future generations can experience an easier life. I have seen a combination of both kinds of stories passed down in my family line.

As I bring their stories and my own to the page, I have moved through intense physical and emotional pain to get to the center of myself. This is nothing short of heroic, and I join many women and men who have chosen the same path. Each time I face a fear without backing down, each time I offer myself and others loving compassion and tenderness, I enter that centered place of healing. We seek to tell the stories of our lives with courage and tenderness.

I offer you the fearless healing and collective wisdom that grace these pages.

Tina Karagulian

She

A drop of light,
the touch of sun,
is but a taste
of the fullness
of Her,
a river of longing
finally quenched.
When I but turn
my head,
like a sunflower
toward Her warmth,
my heart is filled
by Her plenty.
I need not whisper
nor speak—
the smallest desires
of my soul are heard,
and I realize
that they always were.
Such love
cannot be contained
in form
yet explodes from it—
human language,
gesture, silent nudge
all bow and yield
to pure intention,
yet also rest within
every weakness.
She guides my step,
ignites my spark,
and we claim
each other
as One.

Tina Karagulian

Descent

And so we begin. Not as babes newly emerging from the womb, but reborn in midlife. In my early forties, months before I was to facilitate a creativity workshop at a Christian conference, I was not aware of the next round of rebirthing I was to encounter. I was in the middle of painting a portrait of Christ. I have always felt the presence of Christ, even as a young child, so I particularly enjoyed having him as the subject matter before me. I learned about Christ through the Armenian Apostolic Church, an orthodox tradition rich with beautiful music that can mystically transport the listener into the heart of her soul, into the center of life. Whenever I work on a portrait, the eyes have to be just right, to show the essence of the person. I wanted Christ's eyes to show how much I felt loved by him whenever I prayed to him.

A few years prior to the conference, I painted my own version of what began as a Madonna portrait on canvas. I donated it to the Shrine of the Black Madonna—Our Lady of Czestochowa—in East San Antonio. Though I am not Catholic, the shrine holds a very special place in my heart, for it was where I first felt blessed by *Her*. It began a journey of finding out who she really is for me. Is she Mary? Is she more than that? Is she part of God somehow? The God I had always known is a loving and balanced figure, with both female and male attributes, yet for some reason unknown to me, seeing my Creator as Feminine started making its way into my consciousness.

I knew that God could not be limited in any way, in name or in attributes. Our Creator is pure loving energy, our source and essence, alive within us if we are willing to connect. Yet, at times we need to make the active choice to claim that divinity, to claim that relationship, in whatever way we need at a given time. Whatever moves us closer to who we really are, who we are meant to be.

Pat and I did not know the impact *She* would have on our lives when we strolled in the Black Madonna shrine years ago. We had just made a commitment to be together and decided to go to San Antonio to visit the missions and the shrine. The building we were in was the original church at that time; you could feel the years and years of prayers that soaked up the walls, prayers given up by all the people who had visited before us. Photographs of loved ones were left at the base of statues of Mary, petitions made by devout followers. But the most striking image was the portrait of a dark-skinned Mary with a gash on her cheek. She had a face of strength and held her child close to her. Some legends say that she became dark-skinned by a fire; some say that she survived slashes to her face after a theft. What remained was a woman who showed that suffering on her body would not stop her role as a mother and as a leader.

We are called to enter fires of suffering in order to get to the other side, in order to be reborn to our true souls. The Black Madonna is dark-skinned—she lives in the shadows of our consciousness, yet she is stirring many of us back to who we are. Little did Pat and I know we were being claimed by that sacred feminine source that lives inside each of us—a source that also links us to Mother Earth, and to each person and animal around us.

When we walked into the Black Madonna shrine, the Polish nuns were getting ready for a church service. Their white hair glistened and their peaceful energy filled the room. For a moment, we sat in chairs at the very back of the church. Pat said that the blue light from the stained glass behind us shone brightly on my head, like a projector beaming a prism of light. I suddenly felt the presence of angels and ancestors that had passed on, particularly my maternal grandmother, and in my mind I saw them all smiling at us, surrounding us in a circle. I felt their blessing and joy, and imagined what probably happened in ancient days, when people married one another in the midst of nature, standing boldly in the rightness of their choice. I felt immeasurably blessed and was deeply moved, but said nothing to Pat. When we walked out of the church, Pat turned to me and said,

I think we just got married.

I was elated, amazed that someone in human form could actually feel what I had long experienced in my solitary life. That day was the beginning, a marriage of our souls, a blessing of our union.

Since that day, I made a promise in my heart that I would give something back to the shrine, in gratitude. I painted a portrait of *Her* and also created prayer cards with the same image, to honor the Black Madonna, and all She represents—an intersecting point for *all* forms of the mother—Mother Earth, Mother Mary, and leading to the Source of All, a Mother aspect of God or *Divine* Mother. She resides within each of us. I had been searching for *Her* all my life, like an adopted child searching for her biological mother. I had been receiving pieces of *Her* along the way, from many of the people and energies in my life: my grandmother, my mother, my father, my uncles, the trees, the ocean, and the many women and men who have touched my heart and soul during my life's journey. Each person offered a piece of the puzzle. But I longed for more.

Since the blessing of the blue light upon me, I felt something illuminated within me, almost an invisible magnet pulling me closer to *Her*. For many years after that day, I read numerous books about the Divine Feminine. Such books as China Galland's *Longing for Darkness*[3] and Sue Monk Kidd's *The Secret Life of Bees*[4] and *Dance of the Dissident Daughter*[5] helped me realize that there was something more inside of me that was drawn to God in a feminine form, that I was made in *Her* image somehow. I felt that whatever was missing inside of me could only be filled through a connection with *Her*, and that *She* wanted to be present for both women *and* men, that through *Her* we could find balance and wholeness in all relationships. The fact that Pat and I were married in the Church of the Black Madonna was no accident. Our Creator, Our Mother, was calling us home.

Divine Mother

Exalted Mother in All Forms,
Enter and explode my heart,
Guide me in right action,
That I may be your eyes,
That I may hear with your ears,
That my soul may rest upon you
and love with commanding presence,
Within every thought,
Within every action,
Knowing, without doubt,
That you are my Divine Mother,
You protect me as a Warrior
Walks without fear into darkness,
You nurture my soul's stirrings, and
You adore me with a love that
Surpasses human understanding.
I fully claim you,
and I am forever yours.[6]

Tina Karagulian

Surrender

As I prepared to give my talk at the conference, someone contacted me and asked if I had any books or items to sell in their bookstore. I thought about it and decided to offer both the Divine Mother prayer cards and, if I finished Christ's portrait in time, Christ prayer cards as well. They just fit together on so many levels for me. They represented the yin and the yang in each of us, a oneness that I knew to be crucial for me. My spiritual journey has guided me to see that no one tradition or aspect of the divine is more important than any other, including how we see our Creator. Our unity is not just reflected in our personal relationships with one another, but also in how we see our divine images.

I was informed that because it was a Christ-centered conference, the Divine Mother prayer cards would not be permitted. *She* was not allowed to be there. This hit me deep in my heart. I could not understand why, time and time again, what I perceived in my prayer life was not reflected in the world. I longed for a reconciliation of the feminine and masculine Unity, and yet I invariably encountered people who maintained a separation. Whenever I experience a person's belief in the separation, I feel their belief viscerally in my body. Throughout my life I was taught to be humble, to allow for others' perspectives. I learned that I must go with the flow—adjust, adjust, *adjust*—and accommodate other people's perspectives; and yet, when something in me feels like an injustice, I feel it intensify within my body. It bubbles up, and I feel an urgency to *speak* up on behalf of divine unity. Through the years, I have had to balance these two impulses: to notice when it is best to speak and when it is best simply to honor the beliefs of those around me. The longing to speak has always been there, but I have always been searching for a *place* to practice using my gift, to practice striking that important balance.

Sylvia Maddox[7] put words to my longing. She spoke of the importance of lay women having a *venue* for their gifts. Her words honored what I had held close to my heart: that our gifts need a place to express themselves, and that as women we are called to honor our gifts *and* create opportunities for their outward expression in the world.

On some level, all these years, I have been preparing for the time when my speaking would become seamless: less and less about the lack of an opening and more about creating my own path. An important part of my life's journey has been about shifting my focus from what cannot be to what can and is meant to be for my soul.

I did not challenge the decision not to include my prayer cards. However, one of the coordinators of the conference took time to write that he understood what I wanted to offer. I heard something more in his voice, and I believed it was Spirit guiding him. He told me to prepare a talk at the beginning of my workshop, something I had not planned to do. As a workshop facilitator, I have been adept at creating sacred spaces for people, allowing them to hear their own processes and discover what is inside them. I believe strongly in getting out of the way, so that nothing impedes other people's experiences of the Sacred in their own lives. I believe in our direct experiences of the Sacred, for I have seen how they guide us to dig deeper, in order to be filled. This coordinator encouraged me to *speak*, to use that voice that was bubbling up. This was the invitation I longed to hear, and yet the human part of me still felt sadness over of the omission of *Her* image. I moved through both feelings: the grief of omission and the joy at the invitation to bring *Her* forth in my own unique way. I was being given a venue, an invitation. I saw how important it is to look closer at situations and walk through the openings we may somehow miss by focusing on what is lacking.

After receiving the conference coordinator's invitation, I looked at my unfinished Christ portrait; I felt I could not move forward until *She* was represented, too. I knew that Christ would understand the female wound, the need to grieve it, and then honor and claim what is missing. I decided to stop painting the Christ portrait for the moment; instead, I covered a blank canvas with black paint and a bit of dark blue. I felt black and blue and wanted to paint how it felt *not* to have *Her* welcomed. *She* was a part of me that was not represented, lost in the collective consciousness that still kept women in lesser positions. On the dark canvas, I glued shells and collage images. Swirls of black predominated. I wanted to go into the dark places where *She* was, since *She* was the Source of us all. I had been down this road countless times before—meeting a limiting belief in the world that would break my heart. I fervently prayed, pondering what the coordinator had said. Something began to shift in how I saw the black and blue colors: the canvas became a place of creation, not something that hurt me. I then heard a voice say,

You don't have to give up anything or any part of yourself when you speak. I will send you places that you never thought imaginable.

Those words gave me great solace. I did not know how it was to take place, but I let go of the sadness and began to write my presentation. The words of my talk began to flow; I wove aspects of my life and experiences in the presentation, offering the metaphor of our lives as a collage of experiences. I included the beautiful Armenian orthodox hymns of my heritage, my unending love of Christ, and my love of God (in both male and female aspects). On the day of the workshop, I brought my recently finished painting of Christ. I marveled at how all aspects of my spiritual journey and self came through this one talk. *I did not compartmentalize myself.* That sentence echoed in me, for I had said it twelve years before as my soul was beginning to make a shift that precipitated the end of my first marriage. It was a sense of unity that my soul longed for then, and now it was coming together.

After a few hours of quiet creativity, the participants in the workshop gathered in a circle, shared divine images they had chosen for a collage (some of Mother Mary, some of Christ, and some of Nature), and recited their favorite prayers. In our sharing, we connected our struggles, our journeys, and the ways in which we were spiritually fed. I slowly began to clean up the materials. Even though I had been a facilitator of creative workshops and a counselor in private practice for years, holding the space for sacred stories in both those settings as well, something was different that day. It was the first time I spoke about aspects of my spiritual life openly in a public setting and did not feel anyone censoring me. The time for being a passive participant, a holder of space, was shifting now, broadening and beckoning my voice to take a more active role in the world. I had wished to do this in my life, but time and time again something inside me or someone in my outer world seemed to stop me. I had always felt I was not ready, not fully integrated, not loving enough, and I also felt the resistance of some who could not imagine helping to create that opening for me. Yet in this moment, I felt the most amazing peace and contentedness in my heart. I remember saying to Christ and Divine Mother,

This *is what I have been waiting to do my whole life. Let me do more of this.* Your will, not mine, be done.

Those magic words—*Your will, not mine, be done*—have opened the doors for many women and men over the years. Whatever words we use, it is an intention—a surrendering to something larger than ourselves, something that resides deep within us. It is a commitment to the kind of love we can bring into our bodies. I did not know then that I was stepping more resolutely into my call—birthing a voice that had long held back. Something was guiding the entire process. Our traditions and spiritual practices are stepping stones to a place where we free fall, not into distractions but toward our centers. It isn't easy to tell the difference as we are being recalibrated, but if we are *willing* to offer up anything that gets in the way of our soul's calling, the willingness to give up the attachment to seeing ourselves in a certain way, something begins to shift. The willingness to go into the shadow, the dark woods, the inner heart *and not give up* will finally reunite us with our souls. The best parts of us increase, and the parts we do not need either burn off or naturally fade away.

That was the beginning of a rollercoaster ride that turned my life upside down and catapulted me into a midlife awakening, bridging unconscious aspects that had not had a chance to surface, parts exiled long ago into the shadows, but now hungering to be seen and dealt with. Carl Gustav Jung writes about the shadow within, and how when we bring those aspects of ourselves to light, to consciousness, we can then understand who we really are. The shadows within us never leave us until they are addressed, acknowledged, and given healthy expression. Jung writes

. . . if we are able to see our own shadow and can bear knowing about it, then a small part of the problem has already been solved: we have brought up the personal unconscious. The shadow is a living part of the personality and therefore wants to live with it in some form. It cannot be argued out of existence or rationalized into harmlessness . . . The meeting with oneself is, at first, the meeting with one's own shadow . . . one must learn to know oneself in order to know who one is.[8]

If we can bear knowing it was a key for me, for it involved another round of courage. I yearned for more clarity about this process that was unraveling before me. Jodi Roberts has taught me a great deal about shadow, describing it as

. . . going deep within our inner world—our inner cave to embrace the dark and find our light—our gold. The emergence back into the world brings greater clarity and skills on our path of service, in the infinite ways we manifest our gifts.[9]

One of her statements stuck with me like no other:

Our greatest gift is in our perceived greatest weakness.

It took me a long time to dig deeper, to shift through my perceived weaknesses. I have believed that my extreme sensitivity has prevented me from being more present in the world. There have been times I have allowed collective and internal fears to stop the natural unfolding of my voice in the world; as a consequence, I have held back what my sensitivity has allowed me to see. I have also believed that when I spoke truths that were not accepted, something was wrong with me, somehow my voice *caused* suffering. It took me years to recognize that many times I have spoken truth with the intent to *relieve* suffering, even if my delivery was not as loving as I had hoped, or fully understood by others. Ona Banks Barnes has taught me how to navigate prejudice and cultural oppression with love that is mixed with truth. She often has affirmed:

Speaking truth often clears the air.[10]

Truth-tellers create an opportunity, but it is not our responsibility to ensure that others step through that opening; that is each person's choice. But for so many years, I doubted myself when I met with resistance; I inhibited myself, to ensure that I was not speaking out of turn to harm another unnecessarily.

But to understand my process means understanding what happens to my body. Because of my sensitivity, there are times I experience a painful moment in my body, so that I can move through it, so that it will not remain in my family line, so that I can understand every facet of what has happened and release it. I get a portion of it, but it can be quite intense. For example, if there has been an injustice that women have experienced, or that my Armenian culture has experienced, I feel that injustice in my body in the form of a memory. It can be a painful physical experience, and there may be many layers of those memories, but once passed through, the experience is healed. In the moment, though, it can feel so overwhelming that my emotions get the brunt of it. I may be unable to speak, or I may feel anger and sadness at what someone has had to go through. This is what people often describe as body memories, but I also experience them for members of my family, generations back. This is part of my sensitivity. Wounds that have touched my family line, and even our collective social experiences, can touch me deeply, too. At times, this process has stopped me cold in my tracks. Over the years, I have denigrated this process of mine, believing I should have prevented the pain somehow. It has taken years to understand the nuances of what moves through my body, and the source of these movements.

Praying to God to give me discernment helps me not to get lost in my experiences; I am then able to bring the wisdom and centeredness needed to shift the movement of memories through my body. This is not always easy to do on a human level. Without my connection to God, to Christ, I would have been lost. Many is the time I have called out to them in my life, calling for wisdom and healing for all involved, not knowing how to do such a thing in the moment. Because of the pain and crazy-making aspect of experiences, I have often believed that I am not balanced enough, or centered enough, or wise enough to speak truth to others. Many times I am not understood, and I have prayed for the time when God would make me centered or clear enough to calmly speak my truth when the time was right. It has been a lifelong process of healing.

When I feel the most pain, and even if I say something in the moment that is rife with emotion, after a moment of prayer I can often see clearly; then I can bring healing to the moment through some form of action. It may be praying for everyone involved—those who caused harm to others and those who experienced the harm. It may be apologizing for my own misstep, thereby creating the healing and forgiveness through my body. It may also be crying out the emotions and experiencing pain, so that I or someone else in my family line can be freed from that pain. For many years, I had to discern whether I was taking on energy and pain that were not mine to take on. At times, I have. Many of us have been taught that to truly love someone, we must give to them unconditionally. There are no boundaries to that love. I have had to understand the nuances of that giving throughout my life, discerning when giving may *not* be the best in a situation, or the best outcome for someone else's growth.

But I also know some experiences that I am meant to feel—my experiences as a child, and ancestral beliefs that have been passed down through my body. I have had to learn that I am more than these experiences, while allowing memories to be felt and expressed through me. When I can allow all this to move through me without holding onto it, I feel a huge space open up in my body, as a huge healing takes place.

This entire process—what happens through my body physically and emotionally, the sensitivity and the expression of my voice—I have deemed to be my greatest perceived weakness.

My desire has been to be a loving voice in the world: a voice for those who have suffered, but also a voice for the joy we all are entitled to claim. With the words *Your will, not mine, be done*, my Mother God initiated me even more deeply into what loving truly means: claiming my soul and my voice over and above the deep wounds of my life. This became the key to opening the gold and releasing the shadows it covered.

Although I have had many awakenings and initiations before, the day of the conference heralded the deepening of a lifelong call and a movement toward further integration in my soul. It was a painful birthing and re-mergence that was definitely worth it—but in the beginning, it was nothing short of terrifying.

I Will Praise God, My Beloved

I will praise God, my Beloved,
for she is altogether lovely.

Her presence satisfies my soul;
she fills my senses to overflowing
so that I cannot speak.

. . . O God, I fear your terrible mercy;
I am afraid to surrender my self.

If I let go into the whirlpool of your love,
shall I survive the embrace?

. . . For the chaos is yours also,
and in the swirling of mighty waters
is your presence known.

If I trust her, surely her power will not fail me;
nor will she let me be utterly destroyed.

. . . she will recreate me, in her steadfast love . . . [11]

Janet Morley

Heart Opening

A few days after my declaration before God, I felt a painful clenching in my heart. It felt as if someone put a fist into my chest, grabbed on tight, turned my heart and then started pulling it out. It was excruciating. My right arm started pulsing, and I thought, *Could this be a heart attack?* Some fearful thoughts wanted to claim my mind, such as *We don't have health insurance, so there is no way I can go to the hospital. We just can't afford it.* I prayed to God. Throughout forty years of my life, I have relied upon hearing and feeling the presence of God, Christ and angels in my life. Though I have also felt heaviness from people's thoughts and feelings at different times in my life, on this day I actually *saw* evil beings with ugly faces coming at me, foaming at the mouth, saying they would kill me, that I was nothing. I was petrified, and felt my heart beating slower and slower until I could barely feel it. In a flash, I remembered the dream I had had just a few weeks before. Although intensely vivid and lifelike, I initially thought it was just a symbolic dream. Now, I knew it was somehow related to this moment.

In the dream, I had just finished giving a talk in a large city and was walking out of a huge auditorium into a parking lot. It was evening, and a man who had heard me speak said he did not believe in anything I said. I remember thinking that I could read the minds of everyone in the dream, that I had this ability to do so. Somehow I knew that this fair-skinned man in his thirties was not dangerous, that he just did not believe, and that it was his right, but not a problem for me. He pushed me hard in defiance. I pushed back. I didn't fall, but all the papers I held in my hands fell to the ground, and then the man left in a huff. I bent over to pick up all the papers, since I knew they held confidential information about me and others I had known; it was only right to take care of them and pick them all up. After doing so, I walked on toward my car. I gauged it to be about six-thirty in the evening; the sun had already gone down. Suddenly I saw a dark-skinned man with a briefcase, asking me for the time. He wore a butterscotch-colored leather jacket from the 1970s, which actually made me laugh for a moment; I felt there was something light-hearted about the man. However, in the next moment I knew that he was going to kill me, so I decided to run. I saw his gun before it was too late; he pointed it at me and shot me in the heart. I remember thinking I did not want to die, that I had too much to do yet in this life, and that I had to be there for my son. So, in the dream, I remembered *demanding* that I go back in time in my dream. I wanted to go back to the point when I was picking up my papers; I decided then to pick up only three pieces of paper, so I could easily get to my car and not meet the dark man. I said a prayer that God would protect those who encountered the dark man after that point in time, so that no harm would befall them.

I woke up from the dream in a sweat. It felt so very real, and I remember thinking, *I don't want to visit that city anytime soon!* The images lingered, as well as the emotions I felt, so I knew it was an important dream somehow. I have vivid dreams from time to time, where I feel there is an important message, important enough to listen closely. But I didn't really reflect upon this dream until that day I fell to the floor, clutching my heart. Were the two related? Was I to die? I called out to Divine Mother, to Christ, to my favorite archangels, Michael the protector and Raphael the healer. I called to them to come to my aid.

My husband Pat and I prayed fervently together for help. Peace would come, but it would only be temporary. A few days later, I was home alone, and I felt the clutching again at my heart. I called out loudly to God, *Tell me! If this is a heart attack, I will go to the hospital, no matter what the cost. We will deal with it. But if this is of the spirit, and I can heal it somehow, tell me!* I suddenly felt very strongly that it was a battle of the spirit, and that I was going to be able to master it somehow.

It was then that I saw Archangel Michael's face nearby and felt incredible peace. Some may say he is an aspect of me. All I know is that he is an ally I have had for many, many years. The evil beings were still present, but he stood much taller behind them, in a blue light. He did not intervene, which initially surprised me, since I have always felt his swift presence take care of any number of situations when I asked him. This was somehow different. I knew on some level that I had to do my part, that this was another step in strengthening my voice, but that I had back-up help. He looked at me with a twinkle in his eye, as if to say that he would give me a clue; he said quietly, out of the corner of his mouth, matter-of-factly,

Well, you're not dead yet.

It reminded me of someone from the sidelines of a play, whispering the lines you've forgotten! It made me smile. He was telling me that these beings were lying to me, frightening me with words that made no sense. I was called to speak my truth and claim my right to heal, with a healing power that lived within me, too. I needed to use my voice and my strength to claim my life in a new way. So, I said boldly to the evil beings,

Your words are just lies. I'm still here—I'm not dead yet! Michael, send all of these beings to Divine Mother. I claim this healing, in the name of Christ!

Everything went still, and I felt peace in my body. My claiming something deep within me was different from what I had done before; in the past I had called upon someone else to intervene for me. It was as if I were ready to take it to another level, not allowing fear to take residence within my heart. Whenever people attributed their healing to Christ, he often said,

Your faith has made you well.[12]

Healing, then, is a cooperative process; it involves our claiming a right to be healed of the pain of the moment. I knew there was more to understand, that somehow this was just the beginning.

During my life, I have had the ability to hear the unspoken thoughts and fears of others. I have often spoken these thoughts aloud, so that they can be seen, heard, and transformed. Yet there have been times when I have not known how to transform the heaviness of negative thoughts around me.

As I grew up, I learned that unresolved thoughts from our family histories and from the collective world come to life in those who are sensitive. Unresolved fearful energy within us and from others can garner strength over years if not addressed. Jung writes

. . . there are remnants of a collective shadow figure which prove that the personal shadow is in part descended from a numinous collective figure. This collective figure gradually breaks up under the impact of civilization, leaving traces in folklore which are difficult to recognize.[13]

These traces become hidden from view, but ultimately, they rise up so that they can be faced, so that we can choose to move without limitation in a different direction, so that our souls can shine forth.

How many times, because of my insatiable curiosity, have I wanted to understand *Why?* without stopping to breathe into the process, even when that process has been frightening? I learned from Winona Diltz[14], an avid dream researcher, that when we have lifelike dreams, it is vitally important to examine them, and that no one can interpret our dreams but ourselves. Winona also shared with me the day she met her shadow—one similar to the one in my dream. It was 1970, and she was in the middle of a shower when she felt a big, dark, male presence; the experience was so terrifying that she ran out of her home. She shares,

I got out of the shower, put on my terrycloth robe, and very carefully walked past this presence. I went outside— it was January or February— and waited outside until my husband came home. It was a most unpleasant situation, and I struggled with it until 1981 when I finally surrendered to it. I lay down on the floor, face down, and said, I let go of my resistance. Whatever you want me to do, I will do it.

Within a month, she said she met her teacher. She shares that the shadow can be a powerful reflection of something within us. In the end, she learned that when the shadow comes to you in this way, you must surrender. That statement initially baffled me. I certainly did not want to surrender to negativity. I reflected on this for a few months, trying to figure out to what I was to surrender. It seemed to be twofold:

Surrendering means bringing to awareness my fears and hidden desires, so that all that is left is the ultimate surrender: uniting with the wisdom and clarity of my soul.

Each time I have been willing, I have called upon that clarity to assist me. For the next six months after my vivid shadow-dream, I found myself listening deeply, open to what people suggested, trying things on for size, analyzing aspects of my dream and my inner life. I took pieces that worked and left the rest. I was on a deep journey, with no turning back. My calling began in my childhood, but it has taken years for it to synthesize. I listened deeply to my gut, and I had to discern each and every thing that came my way, discovering what was valid and unique for *my soul*.

Many spiritual directors and contemplatives believe that to do anything during these journeys distracts from the transformation; only we can decide which actions are distractions and which actions move us closer to our souls. The intense energy felt on these journeys can often lead to a purging of ourselves toward more healing and reconciliation; it can feel like a tornado. For six months, I could neither sing nor paint. I found myself slowing down. I had moments when I felt I could no longer censor my speech—much to my chagrin! And yet, I began to see that whatever needed to flow wanted to come through me; if I resisted that flow, it would hurt my body. I allowed what had been hidden to look out into the light of day. Words wanted to move through me, once and for all; I gave myself fully to writing. I found myself reviewing moments of my life, wanting to see them as God saw them. Since I gave up parts of my voice years ago, it made sense that through writing I could bridge what had not been voiced, as I synthesized my life experiences. Writing was my right action.

As a therapist, I knew that whenever we have nightmares, whenever we experience suffering, behind the suffering are parts of us trying to tell us something crucial that we have overlooked; a part of us—a story within us—longs to be fully seen and heard. Fearful thoughts are parts of us that need attention, and a calm and clear part of ourselves can call out what is true and what isn't.

Many of us have encountered negative thoughts and forces. Some call them demons, some the Devil, but in the end, whatever they are, they represent lies that live both outside and within us. Seeing them as fears is one step; refusing to accept them in our bodies is another important step. Offering them up to our Creator through prayer is an important step for me. By offering them up in prayer, I give up trying to handle everything on my own. Offering up prayer to a Creator, and *claiming* that healing, has proven to be the best outcome for me to shift the heaviness, the lies, and the negativity.

Betty Eadie describes a similar experience when she chose to return to her life on earth after a near-death experience. Her experience in heaven was so fulfilling that she had a strong resistance to return, but given all that was shown to her about what was left of her call and mission, she decided to come back, out of love for Christ and God. When she returned to her body, she said she was about to close her eyes and drift off to sleep. She writes that she

. . . cringed backward in fear . . . They were creatures of the most hideous and grotesque appearance imaginable . . . They came toward me, snarling, growling, and hissing. They were full of hate, and I knew that they intended to kill me . . . When I thought I could bear it no more and my fear seemed about to overwhelm me, my three adoring angels . . . entered the room again, and the creatures fled. The angels said not to fear, that I was protected.[15]

It was when Betty claimed her calling that she initially met with intense opposition; such is the case for many of us who know we must take an important step forward. We must gather whatever strength is within us, and call upon divine assistance and our communities to support us.

Christina Guerra, a spiritual director and friend, recommended that I read Immaculée Ilibagiza's memoir *Left to Tell: Discovering God Amidst the Rwandan Holocaust*; she felt that certain aspects of Immanculée's life intersected with mine. Each time I read about someone's ability to hear God within a terror-filled moment, I feel connected to a larger community—my sisters and brothers. Immaculée Ilibagiza is one such sister, sharing her gripping experience of hiding in a very small bathroom with many other women during the Rwandan genocide. She hears voices that call her out by name, wanting to kill her. She recalls:

Every time I succumbed to my fear and believed the lies of that poisonous whispering, I felt as though the skin were being peeled from my scalp. It was only by focusing on God's positive energy that I was able to pull myself through that first visit by the killers . . . I realized that my battle to survive this war would have to be fought inside of me. Everything strong and good in me—my faith, hope, and courage—was vulnerable to the dark energy. If I lost my faith, I knew that I wouldn't be able to survive. I could rely only on God to help me fight.[16]

During those cramped moments, she began to focus only on God. She had to fight the collective voices that were gripping her people. When we are connected to generations of people who experienced genocide, and the burden of their pain weighs so heavily within our bodies, it is through facing these negative voices that we emerge stronger. How do we begin to do what seems like an impossible task?

Step by step. One moment at a time. It involves allowing others the choice to move forward, while at times speaking your own truth. Sometimes it means removing ourselves from situations that are not healthy for us, trusting in God's infinite ability to take care of *everyone* involved.

Following my shadow-dream, I began to look at my life history, *all* the papers of my life and not just a few. I could not run away from the fears that were trying to open my heart. I had to face them, and I had to bring my entire life experience with me. I could not edit out part of my life in order to follow my calling. I began to revisit my life's story and saw how God was present during each fearful *and* joyful moment.

I came to realize that I was beginning another spiritual process of transformation, knowing that my trust in the Divine would only increase. I had to trust that I would be led. Allowing for new skin, much like a snake does, transforms us from one level of consciousness to another. Ted Andrews describes Snake's transformation as a period of time in which the eyes cloud over, as we go inward and allow new skin to take form.[17] For some of us, it can be a physically painful transformation. I realize now that each of the main initiations or stages of our lives— whether they be the natural stages of adolescence, parenthood, and midlife, or stages of releasing old beliefs and paradigms trapped in our family systems—entails releasing old skin and old perceptions, while allowing new skin to emerge. These transformations at times were extremely painful for me, for old beliefs were ingrained for many, many years in my family line. During these stages of my life, I experienced increased sensitivity during my inner transformations, and the integrating of gifts and wisdom as well. I had to learn to trust my inner compass first, and then, from that point, tend to the needs of others. How I longed to give others a glimpse of my world, to show them the journeys I had traveled, but it was often not the right time. I had to grow my own skin in my own time, with the quiet of God and Mother Earth to guide me.

It has often been a lonely road, but my Creator has been loving to me. I have felt *Her* guide me to books and traditions that fed my spiritual hunger, connect me with friends who have understood the steps of my journey, and always, I have felt *Her* loving presence in my heart.

Longing

Tenderly, my six-year-old hands
pushed the chair
to the kitchen cabinet.
I climbed up and reached for a glass,
a container to hold not only
the juice I poured,
but a vessel that would
hold your grief,
your wistfulness.

Too many goodbyes
had been shared
by family members,
often not by choice.
I knew that every goodbye
would hearken back to 1915.

I yearned to ease your sadness,
your longing.
I offered you communion,
with the juice of oranges.

You smiled amidst your tears,
and for one moment,
I believed my love
could wipe away your pain,
could erase the mark of genocide,
could turn your face toward the sun.
But your sorrow was always too great.

You could not see me
past the burden you carried.

I believed my prayers
would pay off some day,
that the ley lines of loss
firmly etched into your bosom
would erode by pure love—
but it never seemed enough.
You could not see
how much I ached for you.

I became witness,
as therapist and spiritual seeker,
put words to wordless moments,
offered a sacred space
for others to discover,
to piece together,
to find voice.

Yet I left a piece
of my soul behind,
waiting,
praying,
for my mother,
my family,
my culture,
to find peace.

I continue to pray,
envisioning that moment
of completeness,
when we can join
one another
inside the fullness.

Tina Karagulian

Spiritual Awakenings

My mother was born in Aleppo (Halep), Syria as Siran Meguerditchian; she changed her last name to Megherian when she came to America. My father was born in Pittsburgh, Pennsylvania as Ghazaros Karagulian, later going by Louis or Lou Karagulian, and at times affectionately called Luigi by a waitress in his pancake restaurant. *Meguerditch* is the Armenian word for *Baptist*, and *Karagül* is the Turkish translation for *black rose*. One side of my family represents strong-willed people, baptizing with words and wisdom, and the other side represents gardeners of the unique black rose. Both my parents are full-blooded Armenians, joining two worlds together when they married. I often joke that I am both first and second generation Armenian, all rolled up in one.

I grew up in the Armenian Apostolic Church, an eastern orthodox church; we were taught that our church was founded by two apostles of Christ, Thaddeus and Bartholomew. Our churches had all the smells of strong frankincense and lit candles, and the sounds of hymns that echoed deeply in my bones. I loved every bit of it. My mother's brother was born Garabed, later named Der Vartan when he became an Armenian priest in the Armenian Apostolic Church; we lovingly called him *Kerry*, a word in Armenian that literally means *mother's brother*. During our holiday visits to see our extended family, I watched Kerry prepare from scratch the communion bread, or *nushkhar*, in his kitchen at home. I loved watching how communion could become something out of flour, with the kneading of hands, and with the prayers and intentions that completed the process. My father's brother Noubar Karagulian we nicknamed Unk, not a fancy Armenian word, but an abbreviation of the word uncle. In the naming of each of our uncles, we fused the Armenian and American cultures that were both so relevant to our lives.

At an early age, my father and his family moved to Philadelphia, and a member of the Armenian Apostolic Church in that new city offered to take my father to church. His parents did not attend church, yet my father felt a pull and connection to a spiritual community, later bringing his younger brother with him each Sunday. Together they would ride by streetcar through Philadelphia. Even when they moved to New Jersey, Dad and Unk made sure we attended church services regularly. As members of our church choir, both Dad and Unk sang hymns in classical Armenian, continuing a long tradition of a mystical liturgy that was chanted and sung by priests, deacons, and choir members. The sacred music carries tones that can heal and create movement for the soul—a movement closer to our divine source. Each sound has a purpose, an energy that creates life. But back then, all I knew is that the Armenian hymns fed my soul like nothing else could.

At night, I often remember my dad kneeling by his bedside, for he believed in being humble before God as he prayed. Dad and Unk also served the community through their pancake restaurant. I watched them make the rounds, connecting with the lives of their customers. I often saw Dad sit with customers who came to eat alone, offering them a connection. Many times he offered people a free meal when they could not afford it, or helped strangers stranded on the side of the road. Once during my teenage years, I remember my father driving the two of us home from work and stopping at a gas station to fill up. It was a blustery cold and snowy day, and a man and woman approached us. They said their car had broken down and they lived nearby. Would my father be willing to drive them home? I remembered a moment of fear welling up in me. Would it be safe to let them in? I looked to Dad, who paused for only a moment and then invited them to enter our vehicle. I listened to every word spoken between them, feeling that it would be safe somehow. As we drove up to their home, the couple thanked my father over and over again. I saw my father's gentleness and service to others many times during my lifetime, and this was but one example.

Unk often was the glue for our church community of friends, visiting those who lost a spouse, offering a ride for those who could not drive, or calling those who were alone. As an ordained deacon in the Armenian Church, he combined his love of music and service by becoming a choir director, learning the four-part harmony of Armenian liturgical and folk songs in order to teach others. Unk also had an eye for photography, learning techniques that Ansel Adams used in the dark room. His photographs of nature spots and state parks were breathtaking. Dad and Unk believed in giving from their hearts to those in their restaurant and church communities; they modeled faithful devotion to God, and also service to others, no matter who they were.

My mother created a stable environment at home, cooking meals that filled our home with the smells of warmth. Cooking was her gift; she said she learned when she came to America, watching other women. That was her ministry, and she often gave her neighbors cake or bread to thank them for providing some sort of service for her. She developed her own recipes, tweaking them until they were just right. She was also a master seamstress, from her days in Halep; she later worked at an upscale department store in the United States. With her keen eye, she created everything from prom dresses to bathing suits for us. She was hard-working at everything she did, much like her mother, and she also relayed family stories her mother entrusted to her. I soaked up the stories like a sponge.

Since the liturgical roles of spiritual expression in our church community were held and enacted by men, and since the men in my family all had a strong pull to serve in the church, I also felt naturally drawn to follow their example. Kerry baptized and confirmed me when I was a month old, which is a tradition in the Armenian Apostolic Church. Since before I can remember, I received communion. A portion of the *nushkhar* is broken in pieces, drenched in wine, and then the priest places it upon your tongue. You swallow it whole, another representation of the unity of our human and divine aspects in Christ. This is the integration that I always experienced within my body, a peaceful presence in and around me after taking communion. It came alive for me—it was a bit of home somehow. I always felt a connection with Christ, and it was a connection that no one had to explain or teach me. I never needed an intermediary to convince me of his existence or purpose. Christ's presence seemed more vibrant to me after I took communion, when I sang the hymns of the Armenian Church, and when I prayed.

As a child, I had many little calls along the way. Once, when I was about five or six years old, we had just finished the church service in our church in Philadelphia, and our parish priest was taking someone on a tour of the building. He began by showing a male visitor the *bema*, a raised area surrounding the altar that was set back from the rest of the church. One had to climb a few steps to walk up to the *bema*, and in the center was a marble altar in pink, with a painting of Mother Mary holding the infant Jesus. I often stared at the painting, smelling lit candles and incense wafting up around me. I was drawn to Christ like a magnet and longed to get closer. That day I intuitively followed the priest and the man toward the steps. I *had* to get closer somehow. But the priest turned to me and said,

Girls are not allowed on the altar.

He continued speaking with the visitor, his back again facing me, explaining the purpose of the room to the side. I stopped in my tracks. I know my parents were there. I could not speak; I wondered why others could not speak to the pain I felt in my heart. What stayed with me was that this was the way it was, and it made no sense. This priest that I trusted, who reminded me of Kerry, who would always smile at me and look lovingly at me, was telling me that I wasn't included. What was this world all about? I did not understand. That was the first of many times when someone held a *Stop* sign in front of me.

Yet, God did not stop calling me. At that time in my life, I was taught that God was Father, a male presence, but He never felt punitive to me. There was a remembrance of a Oneness I felt long before this life. I often talked to Him, and continued to develop a relationship with Him. My spiritual side hungered for connection, no matter what, and I needed a way to express that connection.

Տէր իմ Աստուած, Տէր բարերար
դու պահպանէ մեզ այս գիշեր:
Տուր հօրս եւ մօրս կեանք երկար
ու երջանիկ հանգիստ օրեր:
Քու սուրբ հրեշտակդ մեր մօտէն
չհեռանայ ամենեւին,
այլ միշտ պահէ փորձանքներէն
եւ արթնցնէ մեզ զուարթագին:

Ամէն:[18]

As truly as God is our Father, so truly is God our Mother . . .[19]

Julian of Norwich

Prayers

My mother taught us prayers that she learned from her mother. All of us daughters would meet in one bedroom at night to recite the Lord's Prayer in Armenian, followed by naming each family member individually, adding the word *baheh* after each name. *Baheh* means *keep* or *care for*, and we asked God to keep watch over and care for each person, ending our prayer with *poloruh bahe, Amen*. I love that last line of our prayer, for we said it with such gusto, praying for everyone in the world. It spoke to our human interconnectedness, the unity of us all.

My mother told me later that she also recited the following prayer each night, too, a prayer that she learned at the Sahagian School in Halep. Once in a while I would hear her say it when she felt an extra prayer was needed. She later revised the original prayer to include a line about her children and grandchildren. Here is the transliteration and the translation of her revised prayer:

Der eem Asdvadz, Der Parerar,
too bahbahneh mez ays kishehr:
Door horus yev morus,
Dzavagneroos yev torneegneroos gyank yergar
yev yerchanig hankisd orer:
Koo soorp hreshdagt mer mohden
chherana amenevin,
ayl mishd baheh portsanknerern
vor artuntsneh mez zvartakeen:

Amen.

My Lord God, Good Lord,
protect us this night.
Give my father and my mother,
children and grandchildren long life,
and blessed and comfortable days.
Grant that your holy angels

will not be far from us.
Always keep us from temptation
and grant that we may awake
with joy in the morning.

Amen.[20]

I also began to learn how to recite prayers in new ways. I was taught to pray by a guiding *presence*. I did not name it—I just felt one with it, and it would breathe life into me, something inside me that nourished me. At age nine, I remember certain events that strengthened my faith and spirituality.

That spring, I planted some flower seeds in a tiny container. My mother was always good at gardening, so I asked her for seeds of my own. I carefully planted them, placing the container in the window so it would have plenty of sun, and watered it whenever it was dry. Behold! Beautiful flowers of different colors began to emerge from the dirt—I was ecstatic!

Then, one day, I noticed that the plant fell over. It looked dead somehow. The soil wasn't dry or too wet. I was immediately concerned and told my mother about it. She said she would take care of it the following day. That night, I prayed and prayed like I had never prayed before. I asked God to tend to the beautiful plant, to give it life again.

The next morning, it stood upright, shining at the sun! I was amazed. I asked my mother if she had done anything to restore it to life. Did she tie a stick to it during the night, so it would grow tall again? She said no, she hadn't had the chance to touch it. I *knew* then that God answered my prayer, and I was thrilled!

I immediately began testing the reach of my prayers, deciding to pray to God to change my appearance. I prayed fervently again, but when I looked at myself in the mirror the next morning, I did not change. Something inside me then told me that you cannot just pray for *anything*, that vain prayers were not the right prayers. You could pray for someone or something with a pure heart, without looking for a particular result or for something in return. There was something special about prayer, and I couldn't just play around with it. I knew that if there was something deep in my heart, that if I prayed from that pure place, God would listen. I wouldn't always get my prayers answered like I did with the flower, but I knew that my prayer would be heard nonetheless. That brought me great comfort, and my faith continued to strengthen.

That Sunday, I told my Sunday School teacher about the miracle of the plant, sure that she would know and support the wonders of what God can do for us, but I noticed that she did not seem to view it with the same excitement as I did. I seemed to be the only one who could see the miracle. I began to notice that not everyone saw the wonders of my connection with God as I did. In my naïveté and innocence, I somehow believed that anyone involved in church would also see what I saw. I had absolute belief that whatever I offered and shared would be automatically supported and understood by others. It was an assumption I held onto for quite a while in my life, always giving people the benefit of the doubt. But, over time, I realized I had to keep quiet and protect these important revelations. I was learning how to discern what I experienced in my spiritual life with how to be in world.

See-faring

I came from the sea,
much like Aphrodite
in a tumble of wave,
unseen amid the foam;
it rose up,
and I could feel no ground.
Carried into
the brine
of a bigger Mother,
who claimed me
as Her own,
once more I tumbled,
mingling breath
with salt,
until I was spit up,
baptized through and through,
by the waters
of my Living God.
My heart remembers
my emergence:
my skin became supple,
my eyes revealed new sight.
I was remade,
whole.
I tasted a promise
of sustenance
until I am,
once again,
submerged,
reunited,
into the salted wine
of My Beloved.

Tina Karagulian

Ocean Rebirth

In the summers, our family often went to the Jersey shore in Ocean City and Wildwood. I remember the boardwalk, taffy of all flavors, roasted peanuts, bath houses, ice cream, and carnival rides. When I was eight years old, my father held me under his arm, so that I could learn to swim in the ocean. I resisted, kicking and screaming. I was afraid of the waves, but he wanted to show me how beautiful it was, how life-giving it was for him. After a while, I began to enjoy the ocean; Dad taught me how to time my jumps so that I could flow with the movement of each wave. I felt part of something bigger.

The following summer, we visited our cousins at Jones Beach in New York. No adult was with me as I swam in the water. I didn't know what an undertow was, let alone a strong one. I recalled the joyous moments in the ocean the year before, how I longed to feel the rhythm and flow once again. I went out to swim, and I remember getting caught up in the waves. My feet gave way, and I tumbled, over and over, not knowing when I would be able to catch my breath. Somehow, I surfaced, gulping some air, only to be tossed again in a frenzy. I remember thinking I may not make it. I felt a brush with death, but something pulled me out. Was it an angel? Was it God? All I know is that it felt as if huge arms lifted me out of the water. From that moment on, any remaining fear of the ocean completely left me. Ever since then, I cannot pass by the ocean without the desire to swim in it, without a desire to immerse my body in the salt water. Swimming and jumping through ocean waves and soaking in baths of sea salt have always grounded me, balanced me. That was an early initiation, a memory of meeting fear, meeting death and emerging with more than just life. It seemed that each time in my life, when I met with some sort of near-death experience, I gained some wisdom to carry me through, to feed my soul, to guide me forward, and make me stronger. Baptism can take many forms.

During the following school year, we were introduced to Greek myths. I read every one I could get my hands on in the school library. I read these books at night, by my nightlight, since I was supposed to be asleep. I read as if my life depended on it, memorizing each and every Greek tale. I felt the myths had some sort of inner meaning for me. I loved Heracles (also known by his Roman name of *Hercules*), this brave and strong man who always seemed to get into situations that were unfair. He had to learn to control his anger, but didn't know how. Yet he persevered, completing many incredible tasks on his journey toward wholeness.

From other stories I read, I particularly liked Athena, the Goddess of Wisdom, who stormed out of her father Zeus' head, after he swallowed up Metis, her mother. His daughter had a mind of her own, was very strong, and he often asked her advice in different situations. I also loved Artemis, for she was strong, independent, and had animal friends who were her companions. She loved the forest, the trees, all of nature.

Persephone's journeying to the Underworld, and her mother Demeter's inconsolable grief during her absence, seem very much to be the Armenian women's experience—grief over not only the role that the Armenian Genocide and culture have played in kidnapping our intuition and empowerment, but also the separation and reclaiming within our own internal processes. Persephone's descent into the underworld also mirrored my journey into the ocean, as well as each phase of growth that required going inside myself for more knowledge and awareness. Demeter's grief mirrored cultural grief—the grief of separation that is forced and unplanned, or a time of growth that is not given welcome or room for expression. During our lives, we are both Persephone and Demeter, trying to bring together something lost inside ourselves; if our mothers and grandmothers have not been able to reconcile those aspects, their unresolved reconciliations and unresolved grief are *also* passed down. Those women who have been able to reconcile the aspects within themselves can then pass down that reconciliation and strength to their daughters and sons, for with reconciliation comes a greater understanding, compassion, and sense of self. A successful internal reconciliation can ripple out to relationships within families, cultures, communities, and nations.

In adulthood, I discovered that the myths I read were often partial stories, that fuller versions existed that were *more* inclusive of women and their own heroic journeys, yet they still made an impact upon me: women could be *goddesses*—which meant that they claimed something deep within themselves and had a place to express their wisdom in the world.

Clarissa Pinkola Estés tells the original, inclusive story of Little Red Riding Hood in *The Story of the Red Cap*.[21] When we are able to revisit the stories we often tell ourselves and our children, retelling them in ways that illuminate a healthy woman's discernment, important seeds get planted within our psyche. But that is not the only step. In our society, when we tell our daughters stories of empowerment and also *act* upon that empowerment in our lives, we model crucial behaviors for the next generation.

The fairy tales and myths that we are drawn to in our childhood and adulthood often tell us about the roles we have chosen in our lives, the characters that hold us back, and the endings that we truly wish to birth in our lives. As a child, one story that awakened my soul was Hans Christian Andersen's fairy tale *The Little Mermaid*.[22] The tale I read was not the Hollywood version, but one in which a mermaid longed to enter and be accepted in another world, a world different from her own. She did not have her full voice, and needed to be seen and heard by a prince. In the end, she could not live on the earth with her voice; she could not bridge both worlds. She sacrificed her happiness for others. Her kindness, in the end, granted her entry into heaven. This story resonated strongly within me, yet I also longed for a different ending—full use of my voice to successfully bridge both worlds. I knew that she chose a deeper love to make sense of the limited options in her life, yet I couldn't help but wonder if there were other ways that she could express deeper love and also fully live out her life on earth.

Years later, I chose to write a new ending to the mermaid's story. I imagined that her voice was not really lost, but kept in the shadows of the ocean waves, waiting for emergence. The potential is there, deep within us, waiting to emerge. I saw the Little Mermaid go into the waves to find that voice once more, sharing it with other women who long to bridge seemingly different worlds. In the movie *Ponyo*,[23] a similar mermaid story shows a woman revisiting times when her inner creativity had been stifled, and how she brings together many different aspects within herself. The divine that links them all, the motherly aspect of the ocean, nurtures all the women in the story—also nurturing the creative potential within each of us. It is the same motherly figure that kept me alive at the ocean's shore.

You Preserve Me

I rejoice in the warmth of your touch,
I walk forth in Trust and Thanksgiving
on your pathway.
The pathway is aging,
and the steps are filled
with pitfalls and surprises.
Wisdom comforts me and enlightens me.
The journey is shrouded with a veil and a mirror
that we can see through only dimly,
but the Light at the end of the tunnel
Shines forth in our hearts and rings
Bells of Hope, Peace, Joy, and Love.

Lilas Harvey

Role as Caretaker

For as long as I can remember, my role as young caretaker meant that I would care for the emotions of those around me—it was the only way I could offer something back to others. Through caretaking, I perceived unspoken expectations for how to be in the world.

Robert Johnson explains Jung's archetypes as universal blueprints we as individuals and cultures carry inside us, which unconsciously guide our actions and feelings or come through our dreams as images until they are given some sort of expression or understanding.[24] Some archetypes come forth at a certain time of our life when our soul requires us to move beyond a limiting story from our family, or bring forth our intended purpose in our lives. Yet some archetypes may serve a purpose until they are no longer needed.

In third grade, I devoured the Greek myths, drawn to other archetypes to fuse with my caretaker one—I longed to be a warrior and a protector— like Heracles and Artemis—and a wise teacher, like Athena. I longed to bring justice and healing to the caretaking. But how to do that?

Athena is the voice that is able to bring wisdom within institutions, within society. I believed it was through my mind, through wisdom, and through my education that I might be able to bring that forth to others. However, each time I tried to use my voice, I found that I challenged people to look at things that they were not ready to see. I saw their faces, and I felt them push me away. My human self began to fashion beliefs around what I saw, beliefs that were not true, but that nevertheless took hold.

There were certain memories from my childhood that also impacted my newly emerging voice. When I was very young, when my parents argued, my father let out his anger by yelling and throwing objects, like dishes, across the room. He acted in the same way that his father did, and we were witnesses to it. One day, when I was six or seven, it went beyond objects. I remember that my father struck my mother across the face. It was a deciding moment for all of us, because my mother spoke of leaving him. She called Kerry, and Kerry spoke with my father. After that conversation, something changed in my Dad. He never acted out his anger again. It seemed that the thought of losing us was enough to break him open to something bigger. My mother initiated an important shift in our family dynamics, and luckily, my father took heed. There were still lingering pieces of anger from my father's childhood, but he never expressed them openly to us from that point forward. Though put aside, they were not fully integrated, but I could not see that at the time.

My mother also had family dynamics from her childhood—memories of emotional abandonment would take over and at times, we would become invisible to her. There were times she was unaware of her words when they were harsh and judgmental. I longed for a wise and guiding voice to show how it can be done, to show how to break through emotionally stuck places with ease. My father was often quiet in those moments. I was a lone voice in a vast terrain of emotional brokenness. If I spoke up, my words or thoughts were either rejected outright, unsupported, or punished. I knew that my mother was not her true self—I believe she was responding from a hurt place in Halep, Syria, far from where we lived. She often did not remember or have the awareness that her actions or words took their toll on us.

Over the years, I often wondered why I expected more of my mother than my father, when both were responsible for supporting, protecting, and nurturing me. In the memory with my father, when she fought against physical abuse, I can see the strength of my mother wanting a better life for her and for her children. She was able to bring about some important changes for our family system. My mother's intention was for her family to be strong and connected, and yet she could not see the different enemies that would take over and impact us. Each of us has to find a way through the emotional minefield, the grief of a genocide, and the invisibility we experienced. I needed my mother, my connection to a strong lineage of women, to show me how to use the gifts that were handed down to me.

I longed to break through that invisibility for all of us, to bring everyone back to who they really were. Since my words made no impact, my role as caretaker intensified. I longed to bring love and healing so that my parents could remember their true selves. I wanted to break the spell that would take them away from me. There were times I would use my voice to try and break that spell. Time and again, it would backfire. I came to believe that I was unable to speak clearly enough, unable to bridge what I felt inside to the outer world. I wanted to bring healing and love to the world, not suffering, but it seemed that when I spoke against injustice, I was only perceived as *causing* more suffering. This ruptured an important aspect of me—it was the moment I birthed self-doubt. I made a vow to constantly reflect on myself, my words, my actions—I would bring awareness and try to discern what was true and what wasn't. I believed that if so many people could not see what I saw, I had to consider my own error first. I had to look at myself, to learn to see what part of me needed to change, to improve. In the end, maybe it would help my family.

Little did I know, I had a gift for seeing what others could not see, but many times I unknowingly prevented myself from honoring what I saw as true because I had no one to validate it for me. I did attempt to test my discernment with others by asking many questions. I longed for women with whom I could converse, bare my soul, and share my experiences.

The Greek goddesses began to fill that void for me. As archetypes, they drew me closer to a part of myself, and they somehow made sense to me. I felt a bridge between my human and spiritual parts. As early as age nine, I noticed that Artemis did not live among other humans, but felt at home in the forest, and even though she represented such a huge part of me, I did not know how to integrate the strong, instinctual, natural side of myself with the outer world. I had seen so much in my nine years of how society did not accept the voice of women, how the prevailing patriarchal presence still dominated our culture. The outer world did not seem to value the instinctual, natural side of women, and on some level I felt I had to make a choice in order for my soul to come through. That is when I began to compartmentalize my experiences. In order to be accepted in the world, I limited both my voice *and* the intuitive part of myself—like many women, I hid them from the world.

That compartmentalization did me a disservice, for at times I did not fully value the incredibly loving, teaching, and wise moments when they presented themselves—within myself and within others. I saw many other women and men deny their own wisdom, too. Acceptance of the imbalances of compartmentalization is what grows and lives on in hidden places in our lives; as little children, we pick up on the imbalances and make choices that can limit who we really are. I believe that we each make these choices out of a survival instinct, and sooner or later, we need to bridge the broken places and come full circle again.

I came to feel that cutting off some of my gifts and expressing only the roles that others expected of me was the only way to serve others—that I could express my love through caretaking. My intuition and voice went underground, though it would still seep through.

When a person loses one of the five senses, another sense increases in magnitude to account for that loss. Similarly, when I could not find outward models to guide me, I felt divine wisdom and presence come to me in other forms: when I walked outside and climbed trees; through the books I read; through my active prayer life; and through the hymns of the church. Whenever I had a spiritual thirst, it would be quenched in the way that I needed it at the time. I accepted the limitations of the earthly life I could not control.

I focused on the richness of my childhood then, and I can still see those memories come alive before me: outings at the local lake, the Jersey shore, nature parks, church picnics, and family gatherings. Dad taught me how to throw a knuckleball and hit a baseball. Mom would cook for huge Armenian gatherings. There were many good times. We were cared for and had plenty to eat and a roof over our heads, guarantees that were not always there for my parents: my father grew up during the Depression in Pennsylvania, and my mother grew up as a refugee in Syria after the Armenian Genocide. I know my parents gave me more than they were given, and I know that they both loved me with a deep love. I decided to look beyond words and events in order to embrace their love.

During my childhood, my best friend lived next door; she and my younger sister and I would play and run, planning the next sleepover. *Red light/green light*, *Mother May I*, tag, bike riding, skateboarding, swimming—these were our daily activities.

Yet, my favorite times of all were when I would wander outside by myself. The air filled me with peace. I often felt safer outside than inside my home. I would ride my bicycle all over the neighborhood, or climb the tree at school and rest in its branches. The quiet smell of the morning air always felt like more than just oxygen. The call of the birds, the flutter of butterflies, and the softness of caterpillars were constants for me, and I felt loved by the spirit of the trees. They were alive to me, and they sustained me. I felt the same peace and acceptance in nature as I did during my prayer time. Mother Earth nurtured me whenever I needed to feel the completeness of my soul. I relished these moments because I knew that my every thought and intention was somehow seen, that I did not fight to be understood. I felt fully accepted and loved.

When I was in fifth grade, I stayed after school to help paint a set for an upcoming school play, and I began to chat with a girl from my class. We talked while we painted, when suddenly she exclaimed, *You're kinda nice!* I wondered why she was so surprised. She went on to say, *Well, the other kids said you were kinda weird—that you talked to trees!* I was taken aback. It never occurred to me that other people did not talk to trees.

People in church and in school did not see or understand my spiritual life. When I walked and communed in nature, it was what kept me centered and grounded. The outer world of people did not make as much sense to me as the one I experienced when I was alone. Even though I still received love and nurturing from Mother Earth, I felt I had to hide my natural reactions, my revelations, and my experiences in order to be a part of the human world around me. There it was again: another time that my inner and outer lives did not match, and I felt the pain of not being able to express myself fully in the world. I did not want to give up my Artemis for Athena—I wanted them both. But it felt painful each time I tried to bridge the two. The chasm kept growing within me until I made the painful choice to keep an important part of myself silent. And yet, however hard I tried to hide my voice and my inner life, it inevitably spilled out when I least expected it.

Church seemed to be the one place where I was among others who outwardly prayed and sang to God and Christ. I took whatever I could get. The Armenian Apostolic Church and its community became the place for my outward spiritual expression. I put all my eggs in that basket.

The Right of Your Passage

Taste the next step,
into the wonder of soul-knowing,
the peaceful strength,
the confidence of self,
the excitement of adventures yet in store;
This is what awaits you,
you are shorn of all that did not fulfill you,
and your presence in our lives
is a pure and sweet blessing.
Continue to share your journey with us,
for we are ever grateful for the beauty that is you.

Tina Karagulian

Deepening Prayer: Releasing Outcome

When I entered middle school, I learned more about how the types of prayers we speak can make an impact on those in the world. Kerry went through a horrible bout of cancer, and he suffered for three years. We often prayed for him to have no pain, for God to help him heal.

One of my mother's intuitive gifts is her prophetic dreams. It is a family trait, so I wondered whether her mother also had the gift. When my mother dreams about someone who has passed on, and the person in the dream gives her something, it is a blessing somehow; but, if the person tries to take something from her, it means that someone is going to die. I never knew how she knew this, but it always seemed to be true. My mother said that before she got married, her father, who had already passed on, came to her in a dream, bearing a bird nest filled with three eggs. My mother said he was telling her she would have three children, and she ended up having three daughters. When I think back on that dream, I realize how powerful it is that my grandfather is the one holding the nest. He lost three of his daughters during his lifetime, terrible losses for anyone to endure, so he heralded a blessing of what was to come.

When my mother dreamt about someone who had passed over, my cousins always asked, *Alright, who's going to die now?* Yet this time it was Kerry's wife, my Aunt Yefkin, who had a prophetic dream during Kerry's illness. My aunt recalls, *I just saw your grandmother in my dream. She wanted to take her son away, but I told her* No, *and she went away empty-handed.* Kerry had pneumonia then, and I have no doubt that my aunt prevented his passing at the time.

Further along in Kerry's illness, my mother shared with us a vivid dream about him. She said he put two life insurance policies in her hand, and when she awoke, she didn't know if he would die in two days or two weeks. One night as I prayed for Kerry's continued health, I felt very strongly that we *had* to pray a different prayer for him. There was always some internal *knowing*, a guidance inside me showing me the right thing to do in a situation, to take care of someone, or of what to say. The guidance continued to teach me what I began to learn at age nine, when I learned about the types of prayer. I told my mother that I somehow knew that we shouldn't pray for Kerry to live, that somehow it would hurt him to continue praying that way; we had to pray for what God wanted for him. My mother changed her prayer, as did we all, and Kerry passed away soon after.

I learned that there are times we hold people back by our prayers. Only when we let go and let God guide the process will the best possible outcome present itself.

Up until that point, I know that our prayers had kept him alive. Time and again, I was struck by the power of prayer. When Kerry did die, sure enough, it was two weeks after my mother's prophetic dream.

Losing Kerry was quite devastating to us all. He was a father figure to my mother, and his death triggered all the losses that her side of the family endured since the Armenian Genocide. I also missed him, for I felt so connected to him, to his spiritual path, and to his love of our entire family. I remember his teaching us *moderation in everything:* if we devote too much to the joy of living or too much to the pursuit of deeper spiritual meaning, we can easily become unbalanced. I walked in my backyard, full of deep sadness, wondering where he was and wishing I could speak to him once again. Suddenly, a beautiful, yellow butterfly came out of nowhere and landed on my shoulder. I felt it was a message, telling me he was well and not to worry. It brought me great comfort. Soon after, I had a dream in which I saw Kerry glowing in white, healthy and strong. He was in his priest vestments and he bent down to give me communion at church. He smiled at me with his eyes, completely healthy in his body. I knew he wasn't in pain anymore, and seeing him with my own eyes in the dream, I felt content.

It was much later in life that I felt the impact of what Kerry represented to our family—it was Kerry who worked to bring all his family members to America, including his parents. He represented wisdom and vision, a spiritual leader and guide, and without my consciously realizing it, he became an important symbol of my soul's yearning. The priesthood represented an archetype I had accepted for myself without consciously knowing it.

At age fourteen, I attended an Armenian sports camp in Connecticut. I did not want to go. Although I loved sports, I spent a miserable first day running around for hours; the camp leaders said it was mandatory to participate in every single sport they offered. After the first day, we could narrow down our choices to two sports activities during our stay. I decided on swimming and tennis, but that night in the dorm, as I lay alone in my bed, far from family members, I remembered praying to God, asking why I was there. I was so very sad. Suddenly, the room lit up with an incredible light; I was held in a loving embrace, and I knew that I would be fine somehow, that I would be taken care of in every way I needed. An incredible peace filled my heart.

During that week at camp, whenever I wasn't playing tennis or swimming, I sought out a female counselor, a woman to whom I felt deeply connected. I posed all sorts of spiritual questions to her. I felt the week was not a loss after all, that something was awakened in me that kept me going on my path. At the end of the camp, there was an awards ceremony. I was given a statue with a cross on it, and the inscription written under it read *Primate's Award.* What a silly name, I thought! The bishop of our diocese, who had the title of Primate, was on hand to deliver the award. I was chosen over a young man who sat beside me, and he looked at me with a flash of anger in his eyes, saying, *I was supposed to get that award!* I found out later in life he became a priest, and he was the youngest in a long line of priests in his family; he just assumed he would receive the award. However, that day, the actual award did not mean anything to me; what filled me was the knowledge that God loved me and was going to be with me, no matter what. I was not invisible to my Creator.

A few years later, at age sixteen, something drew me to sing in the church choir. I dropped out of our church Sunday School, and immediately felt at home in the choir, since Dad and Unk were singing in the men's section, across the way. I found that when I began to sing, I felt a deepening of that peace and closeness to God that I felt in my prayer time. I was willing and open to showing my devotion in this way. The hymns, written in classical Armenian called *krapar*, were a portal, a way that felt like going deep into the heart of God. The Armenian language and church hymns are based in Sanskrit, as are many spiritual chants from India. They bring new levels of spiritual consciousness through their sounds, for they hold a vibration of healing and connectivity that is very old. Each time we sing hymns or chants that have been sung by many in years past, a key is unlocked, and their collective prayers join us. In each hymn, I felt the presence of all my ancestors, as if we were connected in a wonderful circle of love.

Jagadakeer*

Was it fate that led us through desert sand,
in broken moonlight,
      where whispered dreams floated toward distant stars?

Was it fate that chiseled families into puzzle pieces,
led away "by choice," in a "relocation package"
      complete with all the amenities any genocide can offer?

Was it fate that unanswered prayers remained poised
in cellular memory, awaiting release only in the presence of true witness?

The poetry of my fate pierces through prisms of soul,
      Triumphant in the language of true ancestry.[25]

Tina Karagulian

Jagadakeer is the Armenian word for *writing on the forehead* or fate.

My Grandmother and the Armenian Genocide

Each time I spent quiet time with God, I felt that inner listening increase for me, and I also felt the pull of my maternal grandmother, reaching out to me. I wondered whether or not my maternal grandmother shared the same gifts that I had. She was a very devout Christian, attending church services, and holding prayer meetings in her home. Did she know about my inner life? Did she watch me from heaven? Somehow I felt her presence, nudging me to ask more about her, so I could feel her closer to me.

I would pore over the family portrait, the only professional photograph we had. She did not smile. I asked my mother, *Did she ever smile?* I could see the pain of her life within her eyes. My mom said that her mother did smile, but that no one smiled in those days when they posed for photographs. The Armenian Genocide of 1915, which lasted until the early 1920s, had a profound effect on my grandparents and family. We were taught that one and a half million Armenians were killed as a premeditated act of genocide. My mother was born right after the genocide, and did not like remembering their hard life as refugees in Halep. At first blush, she would resist telling me the stories. Yet she would always relent, telling me the stories out of love for me. My grandmother walked not once but twice through the desert, seeing untold horrors. I felt the heaviness of each story, of each loss, of each horrible moment of losing homes, loved ones, and identities during the planned extermination by the Ottoman Turks.

Whenever I asked my mother to tell the stories of her childhood, I saw her wounded parts emerge. My sensitivity would hear the untold stories behind her eyes, the hidden emotional pain and feeling of loss that she could never speak aloud. I saw how the genocide robbed us of security, emotional connectedness and community, and of a natural and healthy life. There was always a cloud of heaviness and grief that followed each telling of the story, and when my mother relayed those sad moments, she was a little girl once more, long ago in Halep. I felt each story on a multitude of levels, storing them within my heart and my body. I felt my grandmother's memories come to life inside me, all the spoken and unspoken moments, and the burden often felt unbearable for me. Yet I felt the only way I could connect with my grandmother, to understand my mother, was through these stories.

I saw the feminine wound passed down from mother to daughter in an emotional way. It takes years of tending, of seeing so many broken places, applying the balm of compassion wherever one can, but also seeing where the wounds lay wide open. The closest relationships, mother to daughter, sister to sister—these are the ones that bear the brunt of the feminine wounds that have been inflicted over generations. Each generation that chooses to be aware—to face the fears and the wounds— gets a portion of strength back for the next generation.

I intuitively knew the importance of telling painful stories, of grieving them so that they could be healed. Yet I did not observe those around me resolving their stories. I needed that modeled for me, and I longed for resolution for all of us. Later in life I observed that stories are often told on a continuum: courage to admit that painful stories exist; stories grieved and told until they are fully heard by self and others; the shift of the emotional intensity of stories as healing occurs; the circling back, as our stories reveal the light, forgiveness, and love that are always present, if initially unseen. Yet, if painful stories are not fully recognized, heard, and healed, they can get stuck in one place, spinning over and over again, re-traumatizing individuals and cultures. Without hearing and experiencing the resolution of stories, I also got stuck in the same place. I learned that with awareness and guidance, I can choose to heal what may at first seem to be irreparable, jumping off into the new story of my soul's intended journey. In my early years, though, I did not know how to do that. I yearned to find what was missing for all of us through all the stories, and I was determined to keep mining for the gold within them.

There comes a time when you face death, at first wrestling with it, then letting go of things you thought you needed: the death of a life you have lived, death of a direction you have followed, death of a desire you have carried. No, you let go of those deaths and proceed with an inner strength to live in a new way, to live without fear. You begin to see the flip side of death, for it guides you to a place of inner wisdom and compassion. What once terrified you no longer does, and you begin to welcome the death of fears and beliefs that limit or deny; you instead embrace the emergence of your true form: your infinite soul.

Tina Karagulian

Stories from Zeitun

My maternal grandparents came from a family of farmers in Zeitun, tending to land in the valley between two mountains. My grandmother Zarman Avaldanian was orphaned at age ten; her father was farming one day, pulling out a tree from the ground, when he said *oof* and fell to the ground from a heart attack. When her mother died, the only family that remained was a sister who married a local priest; yet, a devout Christian woman named Travandah wanted Zarman to live with her. She raised her as her own daughter, and cared for until she was old enough to marry her son Khatchig, fifteen years her senior. Khatchig had golden hair and was often called *Blondie*—his eyes a light chestnut brown.

My grandmother learned to become a midwife and healer for her community. People came to her to heal their bodies, and she would turn over bottles that were heated with a flame, which then sucked out the pain in their backs. Many such healers said prayers to take away the *evil eye*—a jealous or evil thought that caused illness for another person. Many Armenian grandmothers had this skill. Some would take a piece of bread and hold it over a sick person, simultaneously saying prayers so that the evil thought would then be transferred into the bread and leave the person. Some would bury the bread in the ground. Many Armenians wore a circular ball with a painted blue eye on it to protect against the evil thoughts of others. Faith, prayer and the use of healing practices were so intertwined that it was hard to separate them.

At a young age, my grandfather was chastised at school; he ran home, climbed up a tree, and told his mother that he would never return to school ever again. He became a farmer, and he loved the land more than anything. I believe he connected with Mother Earth so deeply that he could not imagine any other life but tending to that land.

After Zarman and Khatchig married, they had a daughter Osanna and a son Partos. When Osanna died of disease at age seven, another daughter, Yefkineh was born to fill the void. In 1915, the Ottoman Turks decided to exterminate the Armenians; at the time, Yefkineh was two years old and my grandmother was pregnant with another child. My grandmother's sister was thrown into a well to her death, and her brother-in-law was killed because he was a priest. My grandfather and some of his fellow villagers chose to fight back in self-defense. There are folk songs written and sung about the *Zeitunsis*, the brave warriors who chose to fight to protect their families. My grandfather, Khatchig Meguerditchian, was one such warrior.

Taner Akçam, a Turkish-born sociologist and historian, wrote a detailed history about what led Turkey to deport and exterminate the Armenian population, among many other ethnic groups at that time. Akçam's book, *A Shameful Act: The Armenian Genocide and the Question of Turkish Responsibility*, pieces together the political climate, the role of super powers, and the lack of tolerance for minorities. Although some Zeitunsis refused to join the army and hid in the mountains as a form of passive resistance, Akçam writes:

Consular reports confirm that when the deportation campaign began in Zeytun in February and March [1915], the Armenians showed no resistance and followed orders.[26]

In the end, the Armenians in Zeitun could not stop the forced marches into the desert. Those not killed on the spot were forced to march. I see my grandmother sometimes, walking through the desert, without food or water—a journey she shared with my grandfather, my Uncle Partos and his sisters Yefkineh and baby Osanna. They also walked alongside my grandfather's brother Hagop, his wife Mahriam, and their daughter Mahriam. Hagop's children from his first wife were Mahriam and Antranig. Antranig died as a teenager, years before in Zeitun; the story goes that when my grandfather's mother Travandah lay on her deathbed, she sat up, her arms outstretched, calling out with excitement to her grandson, *Spahseh, Antranig, gookam—Wait, Antranig, I am coming.* As she died peacefully, remaining family members felt confident that Antranig came to escort her to heaven.

Antranig's sister Mahriam was fifteen years old and very beautiful. Early on during the marches, she was kidnapped; we do not know her fate. I learned that many young, beautiful Armenian women were forced into Turkish marriages and marked with tattoos on their faces—a brand to mark them as belonging to a particular Turkish family. The brand would ensure that they would never return to their previous homes and identities, too ashamed to do so even if they could. Attempts to recover kidnapped Armenian family members were attempted, but often unsuccessful.

Akçam writes:

It was difficult to find the Christian women and children in Turkish homes. Families had been torn apart intentionally. Children had been taken away, forced to convert to Islam and often placed in orphanages. Some had been sent to surrounding villages and the girls forcibly married to Muslims . . . a telegram from the Interior Ministry sent to various provinces and districts ordered that people with no living relatives and protection should be dispersed among the villages and towns in which there were no foreign or Armenian populations . . .[27]

I thought of the wound of being torn from their families, of not being able to speak their mother tongue, sing their songs, or speak of their Armenian families ever again. We do not know Mahriam's fate; she was never found. Hagop's second wife—also named Mahriam—tried to have children, but miscarried during the marches. Mahriam often cooked for the family and later doted on my mother as her very own.

Mothers had either to endure the loss of their children through kidnapping or death, or determine the fates of their children before someone else did. My grandmother was faced with such a decision. Her daughter Yefkineh was a few years old then, and my grandmother heart-wrenchingly decided to leave her with an Armenian family in Aintap, a village on the way. My grandmother felt that this couple would weather the genocide and offer a healthy and safe life for her daughter. Because her daughter Osanna died of disease long ago, my grandmother worried that Yefkineh would not have a fighting chance through the desert. I wonder how painful it must have been to leave Yefkineh with that couple, to question again and again in your mind, *Did I make the right decision?* Split second decisions were made that would change the course of your life. At some point later, people on the march began to share with one another that villagers from Aintap were *also* deported from their homes. My grandmother began her frantic search to find her daughter amid the dusty desert sands and fearful people who walked. To look for a loved one was a dangerous act in and of itself. At any moment, you could be killed by a sword or raped. You were forced to keep moving forward, keep marching. Even with all those impediments, my grandmother continued to search and to pray. Miraculously, she found her daughter! Her child, angry and hurt that her mother abandoned her, turned her head away, speaking only Turkish, the language of her latest family. My grandmother held her close, relieved to finally have her back, to know the fate of her child. She told my mother that there was no food, and that many women found any type of grass along the side of the road, chewing it before feeding it to their children. My grandmother needed to drink water to make breast milk, and without it, everything dried up in her breasts. It wasn't long before disease and malnutrition took its toll: both her daughters, her child and her baby, died in her arms.

People on the marches ate anything they could find along the way, since they were not permitted to bring any food with them. The lack of food and water took its toll. After a while, my grandmother felt quite ill; her husband somehow managed to find meat to feed her. She asked him where he found it, but he refused to tell her. Only when she had eaten and felt revived did my grandfather tell her that it was donkey meat. She would not have eaten it had she known.

They walked through the desert, due east, until they reached Baghdad, Iraq, where my Uncle Garabed (Garo) was born—my uncle who would later become a priest. Partos, his older brother, was a teenager. My grandfather had a lot of financial success in Baghdad, where he held a position delivering items for a pharmacy, but he was a farmer through and through. This new way of life did not feed his soul the same way that tilling the land had, the land his family nurtured until it bore fruit. Zeitun, the land of olives, coursed through my grandfather's veins, so when Armenians heard that they could return, that it was safe to go back, my grandparents decided to take a chance.

Akçam writes:

. . . in the 1923 Treaty of Lausanne . . . an article inserted in the signed protocol concerning the general amnesty. The only concession that Turkey made was not to "object to actions, carried out between dates 20 October 1918 and 20 November 1922 under the protection of the Entente Powers, to reunite families separated since the war and to restore properties to their lawful owners." [28]

It was during this time that my grandparents returned to Zeitun. I often wonder if they had a nagging voice inside that told them it was too dangerous to go back, despite the assurances to the contrary. I wonder where that discerning voice might have been, amidst the craziness of genocide. I know that it often gets lost amid the intensity of grief, and lost in the longing of a gaping heart.

Reverend Abraham Hartunian witnessed the village of Marash, a neighboring village of Zeitun, overcome completely by Turkish soldiers in January of 1922. Hartunian always seemed to be in the "wrong" place at the right time, offering witness and truth at five different sites of massacres. He tried to mediate with leaders on all sides, giving inspiration to Armenians whenever he could. He prayed prayers of lamentation to God, asking, *Why?* When the Americans and Europeans who promised assistance to Armenians pulled out, he gave a final sermon to the villagers of Marash:

. . . Although the Turk proved himself unjust, although the European showed himself most false, although the American broke faith in selfishness and fear, yet God exists and is . . . Because [God] lives, your dead shall come to life. Your fallen shall rise. Your just cause shall overcome. And as the death of Jesus was the salvation of the individual

world, so your death shall be the salvation of the universal world . . . be comforted, be encouraged, and wait in patience for the glorious future blessing about to befall the world.[29]

. . . to the memory of Haji Halil, a devout Muslim Turk, who saved the members of an Armenian family from deportation and death by keeping them safely hidden for over half a year, risking his own life. His courageous act continues to point the way toward a different relationship between Turks and Armenians.[30]

Taner Akçam

Asdvadz hedut uhlah.
May God be with you.

Zarman Meguerditchian

The Return

In 1922, my grandparents decided to return to Zeitun. There was no time for rest or a joyful homecoming. Upon their arrival, another round of deportations was under way—they were forced to march *yet again* through the desert. My grandmother said that Turkish soldiers sought to kill or imprison Armenian intellectual men, and many times Armenians offered up older men to take their places. My elderly grandfather was taken away and imprisoned either for that reason, or for his past history of fighting against Turkish soldiers. His brother—a mild-mannered man, pacifist, and mediator—remained with his wife, my grandmother and her two sons, and they headed south toward *Halep*—Aleppo, Syria. My grandparents were separated, never knowing if they would see one another again. My grandfather was imprisoned in a damp cell that took its toll on his legs, not to mention his heart. After three long years, the Turkish soldiers had no reason to hold him any longer, and all the prisoners were released. Two newly released Turkish prisoners also accompanied my grandfather, as he walked on foot, searching high and low for his family.

One night, while my grandfather slept, one of the two Turkish men told the other that he intended to kill my grandfather by throwing him in a well the next morning. When the man with murder on his mind finally fell asleep, the other man shook my grandfather awake, alerting him to the man's intentions. They both ran away, making their way into the next village. When the other Turkish man finally caught up with them, he yelled obscenities, but could do nothing amid the crowds of people.

My mother, a masterful storyteller herself, retold this story using all the intonations and expressions that my grandmother gave, yet this point of the story particularly came alive through my mother's voice and her eyes. My grandfather had no compass, just longing in his heart. He asked people he met along the way if they had seen his family or knew their destination. Many suggested that he try Halep—where many Armenians had settled as refugees. My grandfather and the kind Turkish man, now friends, successfully journeyed to Halep, before parting ways.

Once in Halep, my grandfather miraculously found his son Garo, now five years old. His heart leapt for joy! Garo, only two when his father was imprisoned, had no idea who this tired, long-haired and heavy-bearded man was, but he happily answered all the questions the stranger asked, without hesitation. My grandfather asked him in a gentle voice, *Where is your mother?* As the innocent child chattered away, revealing the location of each family member, my grandfather sighed with enormous relief. The day of my grandfather's arrival, my grandmother was working in the fields when someone came to tell her that her husband, once lost, had been found. It was a miracle! My grandmother said she just ran and ran and ran, her excitement rising within her. Objects around her seemed to pass by her in a blur, and the road seemed to lengthen with each step. Her husband's brother, Hagop, blind in one eye, held up a lantern to my grandfather's face. He asked, *Khatchig, toon es? Is it you?* Then as he attempted to shave his brother, to prepare him for a reunion with his wife, my grandmother arrived. Finally, her eyes met the face of her true love, and all she could say were two words: *Step aside.* Her quiet words held so much emotion, so much love, hope, and joy. Her prayer was answered.

As the story goes, that was just the beginning. My grandmother had a good friend whose husband *also* miraculously returned around that time. My grandmother kidded with her friend, saying, *Wouldn't it be funny if we both got pregnant?* She laughed at such an idea, since she was well into her forties, her body already going through its changes. Sure enough, both women got pregnant; my mother Siran was born, a lone daughter when three were taken. The name Siran is short for *Siranoush—seerd* meaning heart and *anoush* meaning sweet. My mother represented all that was long gone for her parents—a sweet heart of rebirth. The other child born out of that happy reunion was also a girl, and she and my mother attended the Sahagian school in Halep, learning Arabic, Armenian, and French.

I think about how my grandparents had to pass through the desert not once, but twice. In the Christian tradition, desert mothers and fathers sought the quiet of the desert to commune with God. It seems we all have our times in the desert, time to get closer to our Creator, closer to our center. Sometimes, though—as with the Armenian Genocide—we are *pushed* into the desert. We bear pain and suffering for one another, yet when we look not only with our hearts and eyes, but also with our souls, we can see that there are always ways out of the desert, too. There are those who help us along the way.

The Turkish man led a man back to his family, back to father a new life. It was a gesture of love and kindness amidst terrifying genocidal horror and brutality. I believe God was there, in that moment. It may seem like only one small act of kindness in an ocean of pain, but seen from a larger perspective, that act was one in a long line of miracles that included the open heart of a Turkish man.

Mother Earth also helps us along the way, bearing witness to all that takes place around us: the crimes, the joys, and all the spoken and unspoken prayers of our lives. She holds the memories of all the people who are left behind until the time is right for them to emerge, until the time is right for the memory of them to find their way back to the light. Even when moments seem so final, healing takes place, step by step; whatever cannot be fully healed by one family member gets passed down for another to carry the torch. It may take generations to heal the broken moments, but if we look with our soul's eyes, we begin to see the tiny sutures. If we look closely, we can see the point when compassion moves hearts and healing scars let light shine through once again.

Community

I imagine
that during the genocide,
my grandmother
walked on hot sand,
lost and betrayed
by her neighborhood community,
wondering how
this came to pass.

I imagine
that in her daze,
she could not see,
a community
of animals in the desert,
walking beside her,
peering up at her,
sending her encouragement
and strength.

I imagine
a band of angels,
encircling her,
ministering
to her broken heart.

I imagine
God's tenderness
shining
amid brutal acts,
opening hearts
of unlikely heroes.

I imagine
that for every community
that denies a soul,
many more communities
scramble to retrieve,
to nurture,
and to mend
its severed remnants.
And as it comes together,
piece by piece,
we begin to see
the woven threads
of so many loved ones
smiling upon us.
When we see them,
we realize
that they have *always*
been with us,
that they have *always*
sustained us.
We come *full circle*—
yet it never ends,
rippling out,
melting
into the vastness

we
imagine.

Tina Karagulian

Inch for tzahnes,
Ahn guh huntzehs.

What you sow,
you reap.

Zarman Meguerditchian

Memories of Halep

In Aleppo, or *Halep*, as Armenians named it, my grandparents lived in houses that were connected together, with a shared courtyard area. The houses had flat roofs, and my mother recalls sleeping there on cool nights in the summer, whispering to her girlfriend on the adjoining roof. Women would often spend time together at a communal stone oven to bake thin cracker bread, or *parag hatz*. My grandmother would make *toorshee*—pickled vegetables—and store jars of food in the ground during the cold of winter. Other dishes she would make were *fasulia*, a string bean stew, shish kebab, *khartmart dolma*, and *kuftah*. There was only one room for everyone to sleep in. During winter, my grandmother would heat up the *vermag* or quilt by the fire and then place it on my mother, to keep her warm throughout the night. Whenever my mother described how her quilt felt all around her, I could see her childlike face light up, and I could feel my grandmother's embrace all around me.

Work was hard to come by, so they took whatever they could get. My grandfather and his brother made a meager living by delivering heavy packages on their backs. This back-breaking work took its toll on my grandfather's already weakened legs. Yet, my grandmother was strong and determined to do her part. She often boasted that people would say, *She's not your wife, she's your brother,* since she willingly worked as a field hand and stone cutter. Once, while she cut stone, she sustained an injury, leaving a black mark under her left eye. My grandmother heated up glass jars and put fire in it to ease her own back pain; it would suck up the pain from her skin, and she taught my mother how to do it for her. Because of her stone cutting work, my grandmother inhaled a lot of dust and developed asthma—she was often hospitalized in Halep. She continued her work as a midwife and healer, reciting healing prayers and preparing homemade medicines for people in her village. When the main midwife in town was not available, my grandmother stepped in.

When children in Halep had sore throats, they would flock to see my mother's Aunt Mahriam. My mother recalls that Mahriam *put her finger down their throats, then a little blood came up, and somehow they were healed.* Mahriam also handwashed sheets at the local hospital for extra income, putting aside a dollar a week until she saved enough to buy my mother a gold necklace with her initials S.M. on it. She doted on my mother as her own, and my mother lovingly named her *Bahbahna.* Her beloved aunt used to give her canned Borden's milk on bread as a treat.

Words were also given out as food. My grandfather's favorite saying was

Veruh mee nyehr,
Vahruh nyeh.
Don't look up,
look down.

Which means:

Do not look at what other people have and wish for it, but be humble, appreciative of what you do have.

Despite all they did, they still struggled to make ends meet. My mother's story would creep in then, her sadness over having to work at such a young age. She was often hungry. At age eight, she learned how to sew and create fine embroideries—a trade not only to ensure her future, but to assist her family. She said that she had a keen eye and after a while she had many young girls working under her. The detailed embroideries that she made were so fine that it strained one's eyes to create them, yet the results were breathtaking. When Kerry became a priest, my mother embroidered a cream-colored tablecloth with delicately exquisite angels as a gift for him.

Creating out of survival and not out of an inner passion takes its toll. It can dim a person's heart and soul. Creating out of a natural, organic place embraces life, but many who lived after the genocide worked nonstop out of a sense of survival and duty. Love was always there, too, but it became intertwined with obligation. To tease out the pieces that got stuck together is not an easy task. I know that women over time have tried their best to bridge together horrific situations with as much love as they can muster. In stories of the Armenian Genocide, I can see it all, the broken moments and the attempt of mothers to bridge the gaps with their hearts.

My grandmother often said a prayer of gratitude:

As long as your belly is full,
your back is covered,
and you have a roof over your head,
Thank God.

My grandmother often took my mother to church, the Krikor Loosavorich Armenian Church—St. Gregory the Illuminator Church. They sat on oriental rugs on the floor, and my mother would lay her head on her mother's lap. During sunrise service at Easter time, my mother fondly remembers hearing the bells ring in the dark of night, calling all Armenians to make their way to church.

My grandmother wanted to pass on what was given to her by her mother-in-law. She decided to adopt a young orphan girl named Mahriam and have her betrothed to her son Partos, now eighteen years of age. Partos was very smart and taught himself everything he learned. He singlehandedly installed electricity in their Halep home, and at one point set up a loom to create belts out of material to sell. Karnig was their first child, born six years after his Aunt Siran was born, and they often played together. Partos and Mahriam had three children: Karnig, Eugenie and Antranig. Partos' childhood was spent walking through the desert twice seeing atrocities of genocide and Mahriam had lost both of her parents in that genocide—two young people who had seen so much emotional pain in their young lives.

To ensure a better life for his family, Kerry brought each person, one by one, to America. My mother told me that she had envisioned herself coming to America as long as she could remember. She was ready to be a pioneer in a new world, ready to master a new language. She arrived in Evanston, Illinois on December 23, 1948. In 1951, my maternal grandparents, who had traveled over the desert twice, now traveled over miles of ocean to see a new world and their beautiful grandchildren. Kerry, his wife Yefkin, and my mother all cared for my grandparents. During this time, my grandfather's years in the damp prison had taken its toll: hardening of the arteries had set in and caused gangrene, so that his legs needed to be amputated. Friends and family would visit him while he sat up in bed. In 1957, my grandmother was hospitalized for a heart ailment and placed in an oxygen tent. When Kerry and my mother visited her, she could barely speak, but she smiled up at them. In a quiet voice, she spoke in Turkish, then Armenian: *ghoor ban uhlam, eem zooyk aghavninerus—I'll die for you, my twin turtle doves*. She meant that she would always do anything for her loving children. She died a few days later, at the age of seventy-four. The following year, when an Armenian friend visited my grandfather, she thought he nodded off during their conversation. But, he closed his eyes to a final sleep, peacefully joining his wife in spirit.

My mother recalls that after her mother died, Kerry gave her an Armenian Bible to comfort her. It fit perfectly in her hands, and it was written in everyday Armenian, instead of the classical *krapar* Armenian of the Divine Liturgy on Sundays. Every year since her parents' deaths, my mother has requested a *hokehhahnkisd*, a special prayer service that honors the souls of those who have died. In the Armenian Apostolic Church, any parishioner may request a *hokehhahnkisd* service, and during the regular church service, the names of all those who have passed away are spoken aloud as a form of honor and witness to them. The Bible Kerry gave her and the yearly *hokehhahnkisd* were ways that my mother could ease the loss of her parents.

My grandmother and Hagop's wife Mahriam were sisters to one another—working together to knit together the many gaping holes of their lives. Through their prayers and blessings, they offered hope not only for their family, but also those in their community. In response to someone's kindness, they freely gave the following blessing:

hogh jangehs
voski tarnah

If you take dirt in your hand,
may it turn to gold.

Which means:
Whatever you do in your life, whatever you reach for, may you succeed.

How does your heart speak to the One who gives Light?

Sylvia Maddox

Little Girl Vision

In my early forties, I recall feeling a twitch around my mouth, like I was itching to tell something, and I needed to find out what it was. When I probed deeper, I felt the hunger of souls that wanted to be free, and I did not know whether they were Armenians or parts of my inner psyche. I saw in my mind a handful of young children, all dirty and hair disheveled, walking around me. I was drawn to one tall girl in particular, and I spoke to her. I immediately wanted to wash her, very gently, and began to do so. Her hair was all matted and needed a lot of tending and cleansing, and I did that, too. I asked her if she needed to tell me anything, but her gaze was fixed on the ground. She would not look up to meet my eyes.

I realized that she had been trying to show me something for months. As an artist, partial images often come to me, images that want some sort of representation. For months, I had been seeing hands covered in blood, but I could not see the face until now. It was this girl. When I made that connection, she looked up at me. She had witnessed the death of her mother, who was slashed in the belly by a soldier; she had run to her mother's side. Blood covered her hands, and she, too, was killed. This girl represented what was lost to all of us in our families—the lost pieces of our innocence and our light, the stuck places in which we all are frozen inside.

I looked at the girl and said,

You must go to where your mother really lives. Tell the other children that they don't have to wait here anymore, stuck in this place. Gather up everyone with you.

Each time I have gone to the place of my True Mother, I come back to life. I called upon the Divine Mother within each of us to guide lost parts back to wholeness. It is my prayer of blessing, just like the ones my grandmother and mother also prayed.

Crossroads

I see this moment
of my life
unfolding,
showing me
the mountains and valleys
that I have traveled,
stories that I have carried—
both yours and mine—
on my back,
in my belly,
and in my womb.
I needed rest,
a place
to assemble the words and images,
all shapes and sizes of them,
like multi-colored glass marbles
shining in the sunlight,
reflecting my inner and outer world
back to me.
I needed time
to collect them,
unite them,
and rinse them in cool water,
then watch them
dry out on the shore.
I needed to know they
belonged somewhere,
that their journey
was not wasted,
that they have
a lightness of purpose,
a spark of love,
and a belly of humor,

wrapped up in wisdom
for a hopeful future.
I offer
these blessed gems,
for the roads
they have traversed,
and for the rest
they have found;
they have become
the river bed,
the ocean floor,
the foundation
for the One Voice
I now claim.

Tina Karagulian

Adolescence

The summer of my sixteenth year, I attended a spiritual retreat at the Armenian seminary in New York. I thought, *That's just what I am looking for!* Armenian adolescent boys and girls from all over the United States and Canada came together. We stayed in a huge mansion, and one room was set aside as a chapel. Each day, we had morning and evening prayer, and I remember feeling that same *at home* feeling I felt in church choir, but this time more intensely. Church was one thing, but praying each day like this, singing, communing together—the cells inside my body felt like they were finding true North. I knew that I was supposed to be here somehow, supposed to be fed spiritually and continue on this very path. I felt more alive than ever before. Surely, this is what God wanted for me. It was not a conscious thought, but on some level, I believed that my inner world could venture out more now, could make a bridge with the outer world. I was being *called*.

I became close with another girl, sharing my excitement with her; I felt wonderful. One day I met Archbishop Tiran Nersoyan, who was known as Tiran Surpazan. *Surpazan* is a title that translates as *His Eminence*; *Surpazan Hayr* translates into *Holy Father*. The Archbishop was the founder of St. Nersess Armenian Seminary in America, yet he also had overseen the education of the seminarians who went to study in Jerusalem after the genocide; one of those seminarians was Kerry. After seminary, Tiran Surpazan brought all those young Armenian seminarians, now deacons, to America where he ordained them priests. Tiran Surpazan translated our church service into English for Armenian-Americans in *The Divine Liturgy of the Armenian Church*, formed a youth and a choir association, and also directed efforts to build St. Vartan Cathedral and Cultural Center in Manhattan.

I did not know the extent of his contributions to the Armenian Church the first day I met him. I only knew that he gave the sermon at my mother and father's wedding, and that he was Kerry's bishop. Tiran Surpazan spoke to us with a slight English accent, for at one time he lived in London. We all sat around the living room, in sofas and on chairs, and he sat in the corner, this white-haired man with dark blue eyes flashing and a wide grin. I remembered that he wanted to answer our questions, and also hear what we thought. It was the first time someone asked me what *I* thought about spiritual things! I was getting answers from someone who had spent a lifetime pondering similar questions. Who was this man? I remembered his telling us that doubting God is a good thing, because when we did, it proved that we had a relationship with God, that you cared enough to dig deeper. I immediately knew that this was not standard fare. I was intrigued. This man deeply loved God, too; we had that in common. The excitement in my heart kept rising.

During the retreat days, different presenters gave lectures in the chapel. One day, a man lectured from behind the podium, and at one point he asked for questions. For some reason, I felt that bubbling voice come up again, and I was compelled to raise my hand. Tiran Surpazan had opened the door, and I had assumed then that each teacher I encountered at the seminary would continue to open that door further. I asked the man, *How can I become a priest?* as if it were the most natural thing in the world. He just looked at me and said, matter-of-factly,

Girls can't become priests.

He continued on giving his talk, as if nothing out of the ordinary had been said. I stood there in shock as the world began to spin around me. How can this be? I had been opening my heart in so many ways, a crescendo of feelings that brought me to this moment, this now. There was that *Stop* sign again, but I wasn't five anymore. This time it hurt with such an intensity that it felt as if my heart were being ripped out. Why would I get so close to *home* only to feel this way? Why were the mounting realizations I was having not seen or validated by the outer world, *yet again*? This was my spiritual call, and yet, it was apparently just business as usual. No one pulled me aside and talked about what I had asked, even though there were plenty of adults present in that moment. No one seemed to have thought anything of it.

Something had been chipping away all along, but this was a severe rupture. That is when I started noticing, with new eyes, how girls were invited to the retreat center so that they could be prepared to serve the church in the roles already designated—mostly to be a good *yeretzgin* for the boys being groomed for the priesthood. The word *yeretz-gin* literally means *priest wife* in Armenian. I watched everyone now, with the filter of someone outside, not having a chance to be let in. I was devastated. It seemed that everyone around me somehow accepted this as the way it was. I still loved the liturgy, and I still loved the hymns. I had to find a way to answer that call. I knew that God called me, but how was I to fulfill it? I did not know how to pursue it further, since it seemed that if those in my life could not see my gifts, if I were not given a venue or space for it, then it was too much work to forge ahead. Hoping was not enough. Even though this dialogue was going on deep inside me, I also found myself not entirely conscious of it. What came was a splitting of the self, instead of moving forward to pursue the movement of what propelled me. That day, the rupture became so large that I never fully pieced it back together until midlife, though I tried in vain again and again.

What became very clear to me, however, was this awareness that *you can only go so far* as a girl or woman in the world, *and* what you see and speak is not always seen or heard by others.

I spoke to my friend about how hurt I was, and she could offer no answer. I did not know what to do with it. If I had been in a spiritual community who saw me, who saw what was being birthed in me and had spoken to it, I wonder what path I would have taken. Would I have entered an Armenian seminary? If I were Catholic, would I have become a nun?

I did not completely give up the task of living out my call, but I decided that I had to be practical and find any way I could. Even though I felt I was moving forward, part of me carried the thought that I had to settle for whatever I could get. I found myself looking at how the women around me handled things. I saw that there were women who went to seminary to become religious educators or youth directors. A pastoral counselor came to the seminary, and I considered his position, but I quickly realized that the bishop and diocese did not normally have openings for pastoral counselors in the Armenian Church, and here I was a woman. *A woman.*

I did not have any women in my inner circle who could show me the way. We were all trying to find our own way within the church structure. Some eventually became Episcopal priests. I initially felt the pull to create change within the Armenian Church. I had formed an attachment to its beautiful liturgy, and I could not tear myself away from it. I did not want to leave my church. It took years for me to realize that it was a blessing in disguise, that God wanted me to learn about other traditions, to take a broader view than I could see then. But in the humanness of the moment, as an adolescent, I felt only isolation.

How sad it is when adolescent girls and boys are unable to listen inside themselves, or to understand when they are hearing their call. Reducing adolescence to just a hormonal phase is not enough. I experienced myself getting deeper and more spiritual during adolescence, and I heard more and felt more. Hormonal shifts—in adolescence, parenthood, *and* menopause—are opportunities to get a jolt of knowledge from God, to hear our calls and to divine our inner sparks. In the best case scenarios, our families, our communities, and our wise women and men will guide us in how to listen. Did I know how to deepen the conversation that was going on inside me? No, I did not know where to turn. In other church communities, there are spiritual directors who walk with us on our spiritual journeys, who hold a space as we hear our particular calls from God—but such spiritual directors did not exist in Armenian Church communities. I now believe that I was being led to create and hold that space for others, but I could not see it then.

I was a whale spouting, before descending again into the ocean's deep. Each time I tumbled in the waves, I would emerge again, but this time it took longer to ascend and breathe again. Of all the stories of my ancestral line that I have held in the crucible of my body, my thwarted call at sixteen is one of the most devastating stories of all. That was when my spiritual anger took root. What I defined then as priesthood was the object of my longing; yet only after years and years did I come to realize that the object of my longing was God. My real desire was to be as close to God as possible, to *commune* with God, and to express that communion in the world.

When I did not see other women in the Armenian Church able to fill the roles of deacon and priest, and when I was given such opposition from those I thought were my brothers in an important journey, I erroneously birthed many beliefs about what it all meant: that God did not want me to be a priest, or God did not want me to venture in close communion, or I had to be a better person first, or I had to surrender my idea of a calling to be *more* of a caretaker, to support others in their calls and abandon my own. The longing never dissipated, and I never stopped my dialogue with God and Christ. But in that moment, years ago, I felt called to what Kerry represented—I felt called to be a priest in the Armenian Apostolic Church.

Still-born

I had a stillborn—the priesthood.
A calling that lived and died in my womb,
in the darkness of my heart.
It never had a chance
to see the light of day.
It never had a chance to take
its first breath.
I know many women
have had the same loss,
had to hide the death
of their hearts
so that others could live,
so that the world could
go on and continue
with their plans,
with their visions.
I feel I was born
to be,
to express,
to give,
to lead,
with parts of my soul
that never had a chance to shine.
Maybe the new that is to come,
will use all the gifts I have held back.
Maybe it means
that I am being led
to an inclusive priesthood.
That is the hope:
Born—
in the Stillness.

Tina Karagulian

God may be in the details, but the goddess is in the questions.
Once we begin to ask them, there's no turning back.

Gloria Steinem

Should I Stay or Should I Go?

A few years later, at age eighteen, I returned to the same seminary for a retreat. It was the summer before I was to attend college. I met a seminarian there who told me about an acolyte class at his church; a group of young Armenian girls had pleaded to attend the acolyte class with the boys. The priest at the church gave his permission for the girls to attend. The seminarian told me that the girls were never late, were very attentive, and mastered all they needed to learn. Yet, when the class was over, the priest informed the girls that they could not serve as acolytes. I looked at the seminarian and saw that he was as outraged as I was; he, too, saw the injustice of the priest's actions. His response struck a chord inside me that I had allowed to go dormant for three years. Did someone else see what I saw? Did God want me to follow my call by being with this man? The pull of serving in the Armenian Church had not left my body. I felt that maybe he and I could serve God together.

That fall, I enrolled at Bryn Mawr College, a college for women in the Philadelphia area. I took a few religion classes, not knowing how important they were at that time. One class introduced me to *The Gnostic Gospels*[31], newly written by Elaine Pagels, and another class was led by a Presbyterian minister, a woman who taught from Elisabeth Schüssler Fiorenza's book *In Memory of Her*. Both classes intrigued me. Contrasted with the Armenian churches I observed in the 1980s, I learned that communities of the early followers of Jesus were more inclusive of women.

Regarding Paul's first letter to the Corinthians (specifically, verse 11), Schüssler Fiorenza explains the cultural context whereby women were expected to cover their heads when they preached. The words *when they preached* jumped out at me, since I had not even considered that to be a possibility for women in the Armenian Church. Schüssler Fiorenza further explained that at that time, different pagan groups had women with flowing hair. Early followers of Jesus wanted to separate themselves from these other groups by asking their women to cover their heads. According to Schüssler Fiorenza, women's prophetic power and equality were acknowledged and honored within the early Christian communities, and the guideline regarding women's hair was made in response to the outer community—so that Christians would not be associated with religious madness.[32]

I wondered what constituted "religious madness," and what made pagan so different. In my first year at Bryn Mawr College, I stayed at the Erdman Hall dormitory, and one day I went down in the basement and overheard a ceremony that was taking place. A group of women from the dorm were participating in a ceremony honoring the earth goddess. I did not know what to make of it, yet watched with quiet curiosity.

In the Armenian Apostolic Church, we learned that we as Armenians gave up pagan religions such as Zoroastrianism to become Christians. Pagan was depicted as *other,* as something unholy, and at that time I was hesitant about its meaning for me. I accepted our church's view that it was something separate from Christianity, unknowingly participating in that separation. I focused on what I did know—that I felt the essence of Christ come alive in the words attributed to him in the New Testament and in the ritual of communion, and I felt the impact of the beautiful mystical hymns of the Armenian Church service. It was not what someone told me, but what I directly experienced. Experiencing the divine within nature was also a direct experience I had, but I did not fully see it that way then. There are times we assign words to establish separation, and pagan was one such word. Later in life I discovered that worshiping idols means *anything* that keeps us from the divine spark— no matter what spiritual tradition one follows, and no one person or religion is immune. It may be any type of judgment, imbalance, or point of view, and the idols or blind spots may be unique to each person. Back then I closed my eyes to the myriad ways that the divine can speak through us; I accepted the separation in order to find acceptance within my culture. With hindsight, I can see that I accepted a blindness that caused me and others undue suffering. Despite those blind spots, though, I devoured this new information about feminism and the early church, longing to bridge that knowledge back to my home church, back to the tradition that I loved so much. I did not know how to apply this knowledge to my life, as part of my spirituality. Because of my own compartmentalization, I could not fully see that women who were often seen as pagan were women like my grandmother, women in tune with the rhythms of the earth. I later saw how the use of one word can cut off someone's heart from another's, can stop the flow of communication necessary for love and understanding.

Bryn Mawr College first exposed me to possibilities for women in a way that my family and culture did not. I saw a woman play the lead role in *Hamlet*, which was incredibly liberating for me. When Gloria Steinem came to speak to us at Bryn Mawr, I felt empowered by her words, and I began to see myself in a new light. I was also thrilled when Katharine Hepburn came to one of our convocations; the first thing she said was, *You know the rumors about me skinny-dipping in the fountain? Well— it's all true!* We all laughed. Here I was at one of the Seven Sister schools, learning amazing things, and yet a part of me was just not sure if I belonged there. There were women from all over the world in my freshman class. I felt isolated from my culture, and isolated from the rest of the world. I needed something to hang onto, but did not know what it was or how to begin. I expected to have many conversations about all of these subjects that awakened me, but I noticed that many young women were so worried about getting good grades that there was no time or awareness for those deeper conversations. Part of me felt that until I had the opportunity to understand what was happening inside of me, I could not do what I needed to do in the world. I look back and realize that I did not yet have all the words to describe what I felt, nor the ideas I was trying to integrate.

At Bryn Mawr, I was learning incredible things about being a woman and about connecting to my divine feminine roots. I was also attending religion classes on the cutting edge, and yet I felt so out of place. Where were my church services? My identity was, up until that point, culturally and religiously Armenian. On some level, I knew that my calling was to bridge the gap between men and women in their spiritual communities, that I was to help reconcile the two. While stimulated by Bryn Mawr's intellectual atmosphere, I believe that on some level, I also felt I was abandoning my church and my culture. It was deeply unconscious then, but that abandonment hearkened back to the genocide, the desire not to leave anyone behind. My church and my culture were absolutely integral parts of me, and I did not know how to move forward into a new identity. In retrospect, I was not ready for Bryn Mawr. But the feminism that touched me then never faded. It made its mark somehow, but at the time, the pull of a mystical life in the Armenian Church was far stronger. No other tradition or experience spoke that deeply to my heart. In my sheltered existence, the Armenian Church and my Armenian culture were all I knew; the desire to serve Armenians and the desire to be close to God in the ways I knew were the reasons that I decided to leave Bryn Mawr.

I wanted to go to Boston, where a majority of Armenians settled, where Armenian lettering was on signs in Watertown, where you could see men and women from the old country walking up and down the streets, like they did long ago in their villages before the genocide. As I wrote about my grandparents' return to Zeitun the second time, I can now see that I may have unconsciously done the same, in traveling back to my own version of Zeitun—Watertown, Massachusetts. I wanted to connect to the stories of my people and my ancestors, and the image of those young girl acolytes spurred me on. I wanted to pursue my spiritual path, even if I did not yet have words to describe it fully. I had yet to find out where it all would lead.

I transferred to Tufts University, and I continued the caretaking role from my early years. I tried to fill the void of my lost call with the ever-deepening mantra:

I would provide others with what was missing for me.

My caretaker role would take on a new dimension. I decided to major in clinical psychology; it was an attempt to understand the emotional needs of my cultural and family history, and to make sense of the stories of pain that I carried. I wanted to be able to bring healing and resolution to those stories, to move the energy that felt so heavy, and to learn how to create safe spaces for others to follow their own journeys. On some level, I believed my major would be the closest avenue to expressing my call.

It Does Not Matter

I do not care if men are angry with me.
I am the open forehead of our ancestors
Where the fate of the Shiragtsis* is written.
I do not care who gets incensed.

I am the loner in that place
of sacred love of women.
I am the needy one, near the sacrificial fire.
But all of that does not matter.

It's no concern what men are saying,
I know I've earned my grandmother's milk.
I am the century of women's revolt.
It does not matter where anger lies.[33]

Medaksé, translated by Diana Der-Hovanessian

*Shirag or Shirak is a northwest province of present-day Armenia,
  and Shiragtzi is someone from the region of Shirak or Shirag.

Side by Side

In Boston, I reconnected with Paula Jurigian and Sona Yeghiayan, two Armenian women who had attended Armenian retreats with me. We decided to edit a newsletter for Armenian women entitled *Kov Kovi*, or *Side by Side*.[34] This was our mission statement for the first issue:

Side by Side is a Christian publication to inform people about issues often pertaining, though not exclusively, to women . . . Side by Side welcomes letters, literary contributions, articles and news items from its readers . . . We ask that you keep Side by Side in your prayers while we pray that Our Lord Jesus Christ guides you in all that you do.

Diana Der-Hovanessian graciously sent us poetry that she translated from Armenian women poets to include in that first issue. Her presence has been there for me throughout many phases of my life journey, but the issue of *Side by Side* was the first opportunity in which our roads crossed.

Rev. Arnak Kasparian, a priest who also grew up in Halep with my mother and Kerry, had been very active in supporting women in the Armenian Church.[35] Der Arnak washed the feet of everyone in his congregation in Tenafly, New Jersey during the Thursday service of Easter week, not just twelve boys, per tradition. I remember Der Arnak's wife Violet as a strong and vocal advocate for women; she imparted wisdom regarding the inclusion of women that also made an impact on her husband and parish community. One particularly important act that both Der Arnak and Violet supported was the active creation of a role for Louise Kalemkerian, a seminary graduate, religious educator, and Sunday School superintendent who longed to become ordained as a deacon and priest. Der Arnak created a position for her as assistant to the priest, and she fulfilled many priestly and pastoral duties alongside him. Der Arnak publicly wrote articles calling women and men to claim their right to ordination, and he also wrote challenging letters to the bishop. I watched Der Arnak and Louise—a vision for how women and men can serve side by side together within the church—and I learned from both of them the power of writing and speaking on behalf of truth, justice, and calling.

In 1986, so much was happening in the Armenian Apostolic Church. Der Arnak invited Hripsime Sassounian, a visiting deaconess from Istanbul, to serve on the altar at his church in Tenafly, New Jersey. An Armenian woman deacon! It was unheard of in the United States, so she was definitely somewhat of a celebrity for us young women. I drove down from Boston to see her and mark the event. It was powerful to see a woman standing on the altar area where many of us women were denied access.

Louise Kalemkerian authored numerous articles in support of women in the church; at the Diocesan Assembly that year, she gave a presentation entitled *The Role of Women in the Armenian Church and Ordination to the Diaconate.* [36] She inspired so many women, including me, to dare to reach for liturgical roles within the Armenian Church. We *Side by Side* editors decided to capture the exciting events of 1986 in our first newsletter; we included Louise's article entitled *Women in Liturgy: Why Now?* She writes:

1986 has been the year when the issue of women's ordination to the diaconate has been raised repeatedly in young people's gatherings, such as the St. Nersess Seminars, and where oftentimes the young men, and even some priests have tried to convince our young women that they were espousing heresy when they claimed that Christ's call to service was for both males and females . . . 1986 is the year when we must decide if we are willing to make the Armenian Church a better place for our daughters and sons . . . If we make the decision, then action will follow definitely, deliberately, and decisively. The choice is ours . . . We women hold the key. It's up to us! [37]

Her words mirrored my soul's desire, and there was a group of women on fire at that time. I always believed I had told others about my desire to become an Armenian priest, but upon further reflection, I did not speak about it openly. I had assumed that those to whom I felt connected could read my mind and my heart, knew my calling by my commitment to change within the church, and by my active participation in the creation of our newsletter. Looking back, I was limping around with a partial voice—most of it was kept tightly locked in my heart. I believe many of us were in the same boat, trying to break new ground, but without the emotional tools and experience to support one another.

Yet I was still determined to see how far our momentum would reach. I watched and listened to others at the time, and wondered if the environment was ripe enough for any type of movement or change. The 84th Annual Assembly of the Eastern Diocese of the Armenian Church met in Racine, Wisconsin in May, 1986, and the vote of all Diocesan delegates (lay people representing each church in the diocese) was 96 to 22 in favor of the ordination of women to the diaconate.

I was lit up; I would fight for others to have a place in the church through my words and through my activism, and on some inner level, I hoped it would be my future, too. Unfortunately, the bishops who also met at the 84th Annual Assembly did not act upon the vote of the lay people. The hierarchy of the church made the decision to stop the momentum, and the lay people did not know steps to take to challenge the ruling. Those of us who voiced change did not want to break away from the institutional church; we wanted dialogue and opportunities, while remaining connected within our community.

Though there was no outward institutional change, we editors of *Side by Side* met many women who were excited about our newsletter and who sent donations for our efforts to continue. I knew that having women's circles where we met, connected, and nurtured one another's callings was crucial to the progression of ideas and support of one another, but I do not believe that we were ready to do that within the context of the Armenian Church. Still, at that time, something spurred me on to try and exhaust every possible avenue within the church. I saw an awareness and strength in the Armenian feminist writers around me, but wondered how to incorporate the spiritual hunger I carried, along with other women in our church communities. At that time, I was blind to the wealth of possibilities that writing could offer me. I was a writer, and I was a voice for women, and I was pulled in a spiritual direction. How to bridge that together with a vocation that satisfied my soul?

We *Side by Side* editors sponsored a retreat for Armenian Church women in Tenafly, New Jersey in 1991, and I facilitated the discussion groups. We were creating a space for women, and I wondered whether or not women there would be open to sharing what I had held so close to my heart. I was attempting what Jean Shinoda Bolen describes in her book *The Millionth Circle,*[38] but I did not have a model to follow then. I was searching for spiritual women who were also open to women participating at all levels of the church. The women who came were very reserved, watching with hesitation. Some seemed threatened by the gathering and came to investigate. In the end, I felt exhausted and wondered where this would lead. It seemed that each time a dialogue began to take place, there was energy to stop its flow. I did not understand Jung's shadow archetypes then, that we all—women and men—hold criticizing aspects within us. I had my theories that, given the Armenian Genocide in our shared history, the act of altering traditions, especially religious ones, might appear to threaten whatever identity we had as a culture. To have another culture kill your family members, take away your homes, and essentially wipe out your existence, the first instinctual response to a history of genocide might be to maintain whatever identity that remained. Change, too, can be seen as a threat to survival. However, the retreat did make an impact. In her March 1992 letter to *Side by Side* members, Barbara Hovsepian wrote

I attended the first gathering at St. Thomas Church and was encouraged that there were some women who felt concern for the Armenian Church in general and the place of women in the church . . . these women feel that they either don't have an outlet for their feelings in their own parish or have been ignored there. . . I don't mean to say that SBS should be a radical group working to overthrow the status quo, but I do mean to say that I feel women's feelings and thoughts . . . are being unattended. I feel that SBS could be another voice crying in the wilderness asking men and women to give real thought to the present state of the church and each person's place in it . . . [39]

There was opposition from some of the leadership within the church in response to our first issue, and to our grass roots activism. *Side by Side* was considered a subversive publication within pockets of the church, and we were met with resistance. I knew that our first issue made an impact, albeit small, but whatever momentum we had was not fast enough for me. The only thing that awakened and energized me was thinking about *Side by Side,* the articles, layout, and the voices within its pages. As I began discovering this excitement in me, the other two editors were being led in another direction. Paula Jurigian decided to enter the St. Nersess seminary. She went on to receive two master's degrees, one in pastoral care and the other in higher education administration; she also became a sister in the Catholic order of the Sisters of Notre Dame de Nemur. After pursuing her spiritual journey, Paula found a community of women that honored her spirit and fed her call. [40]

Sona Yeghiayan went to Clark University, where she was given the unique opportunity to design her undergraduate education. She chose to focus on feminism from a social and psychological perspective, naming it *Cross-cultural Perspectives on Women.* She continued with a master's degree program in *International Development*, expanding her focus on women in the form of *Cross-cultural Perspectives of Women in the Developing World.* She wrote her thesis on traditional midwifery in Guatemala, and observed how women used their spirituality to approach midwifery and other roles they applied in their everyday life. Sona shared with me that she was curious about women's processes, how we come to know and intuit information. Some of the books that impacted her during that time in her life include: *Knowledge, Difference, and Power: Essays Inspired by Women's Ways of Knowing,* a book given to her by one of the editors, Mary Belenky; *The Women's Encyclopedia of Myths and Secrets, Women's Ways of Knowing,* and *The Annie Poems.* [41] Sona shared that as a young woman she sifted through the importance of the Armenian Church for her and what she wanted from the church within a feminist framework. She felt her questioning process was a valuable one, for as a result, she was able to better understand her spirituality and her connection to the Armenian Church. The church with its sense of duty, its stability, and its aesthetic beauty continues to represent home for her. She left the United States to live in Germany, and when she returns home to visit family, the church is often a central part of those visits. Sona went on to work as a therapist for drug-addicted women in a house setting, later serving as a co-director. Now her primary focus is on raising three amazing boys.

Though Paula and Sona were led to the next step in their journey, I was not ready to let go of the attachment I had for *Side by Side*, the Armenian Church, and what the newsletter represented for me. I edited one follow-up *Side by Side* issue, interviewing Rev. Flora Keshgegian, one of the first ordained women in the Episcopal Church and Associate Chaplain at Brown University. It was 1991, and she had been ordained for fourteen years in the Episcopal Church, a pioneering act for women as priests within that institution. She was not always welcomed in her role as priest, either. When I asked her to describe her ministry, she shared:

There is no one area, but if I had to name one, it would have to be community formation. Part of that is teaching, part of that is pastoral care, part of that is management, and part of that is preaching. I'm very committed to women and working with women . . . My practical advice is to find whatever type of support networks with other women and men. Form groups yourselves and begin to study and to worship in the way you envision the Church should do. If it makes sense for the individual woman to leave, do so, but I would never tell any woman to leave. Ultimately, it's the Church's problem, and the Church that's in trouble, not the women. If the Church can't recognize the talent, energy, and potential in its midst, it's hindering the Church and its ability to choose life.[42]

At that time, I did not know how to bridge the pieces that were inside me—the writing and the spiritual call. I somehow expected a vocation to open up for me so that I could serve, and that my Armenian sisters would rally around me. It took me a while to understand that I was trying to create something new, in an institution that was not ready, and each woman who accompanied me on that journey was trying to find her own way. I did not have all the words to explain the deep loss in my heart, the immense grief at not having the support of my church community to assist in bringing my call forth. One event that brightened my day was the joy I felt in seeing an Armenian sister break out. When Louise Kalemkerian became an Episcopal priest, she finally found a way to express her spiritual gifts. I recalled Flora Keshgegian's words, pondering the times that a woman has no choice but to follow her call, even if it means leaving her church community. I knew two Armenian women who had left to become Episcopal priests, and if it were indeed my path, I am sure that I would have felt the call pull me in that direction. But I did not feel that pull. Something was pulling me in another direction, and in hindsight, I can see that I made the right career choices for the call I was to fulfill. But back then, I could not let go of the attachment I had to the idea of priesthood within my heart, in order to embrace a new direction.

During this time, I visited with Tiran Surpazan, who had seen the first issue of *Side by Side* and had given me some feedback about it. He wanted to ask me more questions about its purpose and what led to its creation. Because he chose to listen to my answers and to ask for more information, I took out what I had kept hidden for the previous four years. I shared with him my desire to become a priest, challenging him with the following questions:

Who can deny God's call? Who has a right to say that a woman can't have a call to the priesthood?

I know this intrigued him. I had studied the written work of his brother, the theologian Dr. Hagop Nersoyan, who was also a friend of my parents. In an article entitled *Women and Christian Priesthood,* he writes

We have found that, on balance, there are no rational or theological reasons against the ordination of women.[43]

Tiran Surpazan acknowledged that a call from God is a personal one, that if it is meant to be, it will come together somehow. He mentioned that there is a right time for things to occur, that a community and a leader have to be synchronized somehow—*zeitgeist* was the word he used. I looked it up: it is a German word, in which *zeit* means *time* and *geist* means *ghost* or *spirit*. A zeitgeist is generally characterized as *the spirit of the times,* but it can also be manifested in an individual; both coming together can make a change. I read the following definition:

A zeitgeist is assumed to have a progressive influence or impact which tends to push culture forward.

I believe that Hagop Nersoyan and Tiran Surpazan, not to mention Louise Kalemkerian and all the women during this time, were all participants in a growing zeitgeist for churchgoing Armenians, breaking open ideas and concepts that were necessary for them to grow in wisdom. Tiran Surpazan was an archbishop who had the position and capacity to enact change in the Armenian Church, creating spiritual opportunities for Armenians to thrive in America. When my uncle came to the United States from Jerusalem with other seminarians, the need for priests was so great that Tiran Surpazan broke the rules so that the priests could marry *after* they were ordained. The tradition was that Armenian priests could marry or stay celibate, but once ordained, they were not permitted to marry. Tiran Surpazan believed that establishing church communities took precedence over rules; he led by understanding the needs of the community and tending to them, much as Christ did. But who would overlook rules for the needs of Armenian women? I knew then that the Armenian Church was not ready for women priests, and it wasn't going to happen any time soon. I did receive a letter from Tiran Surpazan outlining his thoughts on my call, and it is a letter that I am very grateful to have received. I appreciated that even though I could not fulfill my call in the Armenian Church, he was the first priest to listen to me and to honor my inner process with God. In the end, though, he did not guide me toward any type of call, nor give me a direction to follow. How much more helpful it might have been to have heard that when God calls you, you are chosen, and that the path may express itself in a wider scope than you might ever imagine.

Acknowledge that something important has been birthed, or has been called out of you. If there is opposition to your calling, it does not mean you are suddenly un-called!

I felt my call shrink back within me again. I knew that I had to move forward on my path by myself, with only God to guide my decisions. My church community did not offer me the guidance I needed, which involved an emotional connection and communication that would foster my purpose. I grieved that loss very deeply. I had to wait for the right time to bring forth my spiritual wisdom within a context that would feed others in the world.

Since his death, though, I have often dreamt of Tiran Surpazan, feeling his loving support of me on my spiritual path. I have felt the influence of others who have passed on, others who have a greater perspective now that they have stepped beyond their lives. Tiran Surpazan, my grandmother, Kerry, and my father—all of them have been a guiding presence for me as I have followed God's call.

With years and perspective, I have come to see that all the women who painfully birthed their spiritual lives in the face of opposition did in fact plant seeds within me; their impact is felt. There are women and men who have gently pushed for change within institutions, and their loving actions and sacrifices are not always seen or acknowledged by others, but movement still takes place. I also know that some are called to break ground, seeing outside the scope of their institutions or communities—speaking out while also holding a space for a future vision to flower. Many of us in 1986 were in that latter group, breaking ground in our unique ways. By following our inner calls, we inevitably brought something back to our communities. It takes truly listening to one another, for we often need members working on the inside and on the outside to yield the best results. There is room for everyone in our communities.

In the first issue of *Side by Side*, we had a vision of men and women standing together in equality, while faithfully listening to God guiding that vision.

The vision never dies. It continues to find a way to connect, to come forth. I see now the many women who forged that road ahead of me, all pioneers who came together and planted seeds, starting a momentum—even if it could not all be seen by the naked eye.

I never abandoned that vision, but as time went on, I gave up part of my inner compass. Losing our sense of direction is a transformation that happens slowly, when those around us do not have a greater sight, and have not walked the road of bringing forth the strength and gifts of others. Girls are asked to be supporters of a male vision, or a culture's vision, if we wish to be part of a community. Over time, we may sublimate the inner spark or leadership, if there are no women or men to mirror back what is growing within us. Though it is important to parse through what may be unhealthy ego, girls and women may also unknowingly abandon the guiding Spirit within us. It is important to discern times when working for the good of the whole does not allow anything new or different to emerge. Working for the group is a wonderful aspiration, yet if we are creative or visionary in a way that is not understood or given room to grow, parts of our souls will go underground. For some, they never re-emerge. That is a deep loss for us all. Clarissa Pinkola Estés describes this process, when unmothered girls limp along through life without crucial skills to combat dangers before them.[44]

I was dating an Armenian seminarian at the time of this struggle and sense of loss; in retrospect, it makes sense that I would attempt to find a way to express my spiritual call through a spouse who might create that opening for me. Many women with a similar thwarted call have, I believe, unconsciously taken that step. Yet a thwarted call that is not given expression can affect every relationship and every aspect of our lives.

At a crucial moment in our courtship, I spoke to my mother and my aunt about marrying a seminarian who would become a priest. They both shared the difficult, sometimes painful journey of watching a priest—my uncle—manage life within the Armenian Church. They spoke of criticism they had received at times from different church communities, and during that conversation, I don't recall hearing any positive aspects of following a call from God. Little did they know, I was the priest before them, wanting the blessing of the strong and wise women in my life. I believed that they could not see or understand this call because they did not have the same call burning in their hearts. Here was a crucial moment when I longed to hear the full perspective, the full story. On some level, I felt that since they could not understand this part of me, I could not fully trust that they would know the right road for me. I did not verbalize that to them. I had long learned that I watched with my eyes, heard with my ears, but speaking out never yielded much fruit. I yearned for understanding.

Only after many years could I finally verbalize this story with my aunt. She shared that though they did encounter difficulties, Kerry never had any regrets at becoming a priest; she recalls many joyful and uplifting moments. Before Kerry and Aunt Yefkin married, she said that her godfather tried to dissuade her from living a life that would be challenging financially, but she saw her mother behind him nodding her head in support of her decision. Yefkin's mother was the daughter of a priest and supported that calling. Kerry later asked Yefkin if she wanted to go into the life to which he had been called, that he was open to another one with her. Aunt Yefkin said no, that this is what she wanted to do, and that she knew he was called to be a priest.

During the course of our courtship, the man I dated experienced a similar thwarted call that left him shattered. I supported him by writing a letter to a bishop on his behalf, emotionally supporting him in any way I could. No other priest took the time to support him. In the end, the seminarian made the decision to walk away, and I made the decision that I could not abandon him when so many others had done so. I loved and supported his aching heart because I knew it too well.

Yet I confused loving compassion with marriage. My body was giving me hints, and I felt a voice inside me saying that something was wrong, that I should not go through with the marriage. I voiced my concerns, but in the end, I did not want to hurt this man I cared for—our genocide history and thwarted calls were painful enough, and I certainly did not want to add to the pain and abandonment. I jumbled together the caretaker role with the belief that this was the only way I could fulfill the now crumbling spiritual call. I felt that God must want me to follow another road, that my vision of priesthood must have been off somehow, but I did not know how to fully grieve that loss. It was not the right time for what I wanted, and I felt I had to accept that maybe this lifetime was about giving behind-the-scenes instead. Many times I had seen people make an altruistic choice to love in a way that offered them spiritual growth and service to others. Personal needs were secondary to that kind of love. Was that the course that God wanted for me?

At one point, my mother saw my struggle and said that I did not have to go through with the marriage. There were many times my mother could not see the deeper parts of me, could not understand the pull of my soul's aspirations. My parents only looked at financial survival and traditional roles with regard to my career and marriage. In the end, it was hard for me to discern the right road. My muscle for discernment had been battered for so long that I could not fully sense its messages. My call at age sixteen did not come to pass, and I felt that I was now on my own; the women in my life could only tell me what *not* to do, but they could not show me how to follow my heart. That was my journey to make, but I did not know how to make the next step. In the end, it was I who decided to ignore my inner promptings.

After I married, I felt despondent. I do not blame either of us for marrying, for we both made that decision together. We both had a love for the Armenian people, and a similar spiritual calling to serve them.

Many factors came together to make that decision. I decided that I needed to make the best of it and work very hard at making my marriage work.

Even while I worked on a master's degree in social work, which gave me something to look forward to and a way to use my gifts, I still felt something was wrong. My body always found a way to tell its story, especially when my mouth could not speak the words. In hindsight, I can see that I was led down this unanticipated road for a reason. During that time, a lump formed in my body. I went to an Armenian surgeon at the hospital down the street, and I remembered feeling uncomfortable during his examination of me. He brushed my leg in an inappropriate way, and I did not like it. The lump was benign, but it would need to be surgically removed. I could not shake how horrible I felt. Part of me did not want to go through the surgery. I started having nightmares about being violently killed. I came to realize that if I did not trust the surgeon when I was awake, how could I trust him when I was put under anesthesia?

I had numerous nightmares then, and I could make no sense of them. I did not know then that nightmares can be a sign that painful memories we have carried are ready for release and healing, that our unconscious is trying to tell us something—our divine essence is yearning for wholeness. By not listening to my gut during so many times in my life, and feeling that I had no choice in those situations, my body had to reflect back what needed to be heard. Something was being triggered in me to see and heal. That night, I awoke from a fitful sleep, flooded with the realization that I had been mentally, physically, and sexually abused by my paternal grandfather until the age of eight.

After the flood of realizations, it was dark and eerily quiet as I sat alone in the kitchen. I knew that I was going to have to go through a period of intense pain. I did not yet know that the circular journey was beginning: going inward, allowing for unresolved emotions to emerge, to grieve them and make room to give voice to broken places, to stitch together tears in the soul when each trauma made its mark, until something naturally began to shift, allowing for more breath, more life.

Clarissa Pinkola Estés describes the lonely journey when one lives for years among others who cannot help you find your way back; yet it is never too late, for with proper tending, one can learn how to thrive. [45]

In those early moments, though, I only felt the heaviness of the coming journey. Why hadn't I remembered this horrific part of my family history? Could I endure recalling it? When would I heal from it? I knew God was with me, but I also knew it would take a long time for me to heal.

There are two ways to look at any abusive situation: One of the ways is to say: I chose this lesson for some learning and I don't need to judge anyone that was involved because we're all participating here for the highest good. On the other hand, there's a human level that's very important to include, which is to say: I was still an innocent little child and it was wrong. It's the only time I recommend that people use judgment.

Carol Sydney

Body Memories

Once memories surfaced that my grandfather sexually abused me, I went to counseling. Surprisingly, sexual trauma was not covered in my master's program. I did gain some knowledge of art therapy in my education, and I knew the power and healing that comes when one draws the pain in different ways. I had always loved drawing as a child, and it brought me great peace then. I knew that once I began to dig deeper and tend to the painful story that was emerging, the nightmares would stop. Only later did I realize that any part of our earthly journey—especially moments of intense pain and suffering—can be understood and synthesized through our calling. I believe that our healing and our spiritual call are often intertwined.

I told my family, and they believed me, but they themselves were limited in their own abilities to see and to heal from the abuse. The same blindness I encountered within myself during Bryn Mawr was the same blindness that affects families who allow for violence to occur. From childhood stories of my paternal grandfather, I learned that he was a violent man who physically abused his wife, and once killed the family cat by throwing it across the room. Yet, those facts were not fully seen or acknowledged, for my grandfather would often babysit us girls. How could I heal from this, when those in my family could not see it either? It is painful to realize you have no one in your family to help you heal. Years later, many of my clients shared how they suffered from a similarly deep loss, and I knew that they needed someone to act as witness, to help them sort out and discern what was true. I am in awe of their brave journeys to reclaim their lives, their strength, and their voices. It is a road I understand well.

Healing from abuse memories was the beginning of another painful descent, and I needed time to understand it, and time to go inward. Here was an unplanned initiation into a dark place within me, and I experienced a staggering rawness when memories came to the surface to be healed. The worst part of it was my mind. For those who do not remember a traumatic event for part of their life, it feels as if your mind was erased somehow. How can you get that back? I always marveled at those who never lost their memories of childhood trauma. But I can see now that for me to get through childhood, I had to block out the worst of it until I was ready to heal it. I know that when you are truly ready, when you have the inner strength to heal, that is usually when you remember. Looking back on my situation, I can see that had I remembered, I never would have finished college or graduate school. It was as if my inner spirit guided me to take one step at a time, to utilize one part of my consciousness before I had to venture inward to heal another.

I read *The Courage to Heal*[46] and learned about healing the inner child. I remember staring at my orange hibiscus plant, longing to feel the beauty of life again. I continued to get help from the spirit world. I found that when I had a horrific memory, if I allowed the little child inside me to cry, then a stronger inner part of me would tend to her. It was a three-way process: an emotional part needing to heal, express, and feel tended; a strong divine part that was patient, nonjudgmental, and protecting; and the human body, a receptacle for all the painful memories that were stored and needed release. All three were wise guides in my discernment process, and with increased awareness, I began to understand how uniquely I received information, and how to heal from any suffering. Bodies are not meant to hold pain in any way; our bodies are meant to release them. How you hold pain, and where you hold it, is information, and it differs for each person. Each time I grieved by crying out or wailing, my emotional self felt release. As I brought more awareness to my healing process, as I grieved memories, my body felt more relaxed, as if the knot in my stomach somehow opened up. Each time I found words to accurately describe my perspective or experience, I felt myself integrate the healing on all the levels.

One day, I went to play baseball with a group of people. I often played softball as a child, once playing outfield on a community softball team, and I was always a strong hitter. I looked forward to playing again. That afternoon, the moment I threw the ball to someone, I felt a terrible pain in my right arm; it also began to turn red. I thought that I must be really out of shape for my muscle to hurt so much. After I came home, the pain still did not subside, and purple fingerprints began to appear on my arm. They were my grandfather's fingerprints, and I felt the tight grip he once had on my arm. I began to hyperventilate. It was the first time I actually *saw* a physical manifestation of an abuse memory, a body memory. It was one thing to cry something out, but to see it and feel it in my body brought a rage at having to endure it in all its fullness.

The spiritual practice of accepting each moment was difficult at these times, because accompanying the body memories was also the belief that I would truly die of the suffering. I learned that, in terror, the beliefs we have in the moment somehow become frozen in the body. Over time, I learned not to judge my feelings or my emotions, and to allow them to release. I learned to watch my reactions to situations and to challenge the beliefs I attached to events. I slowly began to change the beliefs that limited me and redirect them. This took years to master, but I found that loving and not judging myself was crucial to accepting *myself* in the moment—not accepting the abuse as the ultimate definition of me, but seeing it as a painful *moment* from my history. I am so much more. Through accepting and loving myself in the moment of a memory, I could heal. That first body memory was frightening, and I had to focus on breathing to calm myself down.

The original memory connected to my grandfather's fingerprints and everything else related to that event would haunt me for a very long time, and it challenged my faith in a deep way. I was about seven years old, and my parents had dropped my sisters and me off at my grandparents' apartment for a sleepover. We all watched *The Lawrence Welk Show* on television. Amidst the bubbles that came up in the television program, and the singers with their perfect smiles, my grandfather Papa was in a foul mood and could not wait for the show to end. My grandmother— Mama—scolded him, telling him to be quiet, so that we could watch. Afterward, we all went to bed. I went to sleep on the sofa bed with my older sister Lisa, and I remember talking with her when Papa stormed out of his bedroom and grabbed my arm so tightly, dragging me into the bedroom with him. I was terrified, felt trapped, unable to move, unable to stop the violence that was happening. Even worse was watching him rape my younger sister, knowing I could not stop him. I lay there motionless, feeling everything that she was feeling, afraid that we would both be killed. I remember floating out of my body, as people often report, because it was too frightening to stay there.

The next morning, while we waited for our parents to pick us up, I remember sitting on Papa's bed, looking up at the beautiful religious icons that were displayed on the wall. They were circular images of Mary and the baby Jesus, in deep reds, blues, and gold. They were handmade images from Italy. All I could do was look up at Christ and say, *Where were you?* I felt betrayed. I knew Christ existed—I had felt his presence all through my childhood. Yet where was he during that horrible night?

Such anger I felt. Such incredible pain. It took me years to forgive all involved for allowing such violence to occur, and even though I longed to forgive, I could not rush the process. I knew that in the end, not rushing would be the best thing for us all. If we rush forgiveness, if we do not fully heal ourselves or have the chance to be fully heard by someone, then forgiveness only backfires. It takes a lot of focus to heal from such pain, to shift our focus to the goodness inside ourselves. I felt responsible for not protecting my sister, for not being there for her. It was too much for a young child to do, and even though I learned it was not my fault, it still became the worst memory for me. It was devastating to see my beloved sister stripped of her emotional and spiritual strength before my eyes, so injured that acts of love cannot enter. This was the defining moment that put me on a course to become a loving witness for souls to find their way back to themselves. This moment does not just happen on a family level, but on a cultural level as well. Our countries each play a part in creating and maintaining soul brokenness: superpowers that model entitlement and land ownership encourage desperate countries to do the same with different ethnic groups within their lands, creating conditions ripe for genocide, which can then filter down to families as well. Each time we make a decision to see others as separate, ignoring the beauty of their souls, each time a woman is not given a venue to express her gifts, each time a girl is sold into sex slavery while her culture does not respond, we all suffer. It takes each of us making a conscious choice: those of us who embark on the long journey to heal, and all of us who are witnesses to it. This is the legacy with which Armenians have struggled in the aftermath of the Armenian Genocide. How to move forward when you have witnessed cruel acts on your family members? How to forgive others, let alone yourself?

Over the years, I have come to realize that forgiving means releasing the pain *for ourselves*. I could not heal without a spiritual connection. I learned that the process of forgiveness is not something you have to do on your own, and that full forgiveness often happens over a period of time and through many levels of release. The healing journey includes inner and outer guides who help us piece together our shattered psyches, as we journey back to ourselves. I knew that I could rage at God, that God could handle it, that I was entitled to healing, and I allowed for that as well. Time and time again, I have said to God and Christ,

I don't know how to do this. I trust You to show me the way.

Years later when I revisited the memory of that night in my grandparents' apartment, I became aware of the presence of Christ holding me—he prevented me from shattering completely. I knew then that many have died experiencing such violence, and that I would have died that night, too. I cannot begin to explain each person's spiritual journey, and yet I am flooded with assurance that those who die in such a manner are tended to in heaven, that the sacrifice of their lives is an opportunity for some healing and good to take place on earth, if we but take it. I have felt deeply connected to those who have died, as if they have passed the baton to me to tell their stories, too, so that the violence that ended their lives can also be brought to light. I know that many who die in such ways are often wise souls who come to teach others how to open their hearts more fully. How many times I wished I could join those souls who have died, for during the worst memories, I wished I could have been taken home to heaven in lieu of having to relive the pain. I was never suicidal—but I did come to the edge many, many times, feeling terrified, mute, and shattered. Just like the day I was tumbled in the ocean, each time I faced a shattered memory, I met death and was resurrected. Those moments when I felt the most despair, a light always came through to heal the moment, to heal that memory—bringing me back to life again and again.

My own recovered memories began to help explain why I was so sensitive to stories of women being raped during the forced marches of the Armenian Genocide. They also explained why I felt so sensitive to children being hurt. When countries engage in wars, do we ever consider the time it takes to heal from one act of violence, one act of rape to a woman or child? Mothering gets impaired, leaving blind spots and the inability to sense unhealthy people or situations for their children. Repeated acts of violence toward children, women, and a culture leave all of us crippled in one way or another, and those who struggle to heal are often misunderstood or blamed. Finding a safe haven in which to heal is crucial—finding people who can see the beauty of our souls, despite the violence we may have suffered. To this day, I am dismayed that we still look at people who have gone through a horrific trauma and want to put them in a box, saying

Oh, that explains why they're like that.

There may be gaps in healing at times, but what if as communities we instead focus on the strength and courage it takes to survive such ordeals? If we *all* begin to heal the wounds that each of us carries, bringing them to awareness and focusing on solutions, then perhaps conditions that are ripe for abuse and genocide will fall dramatically.

The primary reason I am writing this memoir is to bring hope to those who have temporarily forgotten how to find their way, who have felt stuck in some endless loop in their lives. There is so much more to our stories. We are meant to heal each painful story we have lived.

I saw many wonderful therapists along the way who could hear me, who taught me how to set boundaries, and who told me it was not my fault that I could not stop the violence or protect my sister. I made a commitment to heal myself *in any way* I needed, and I asked God to show the way. I do believe this intention is what led me to find alternative healing practices and other spiritual traditions that would bring me forward on my journey. I had to go beyond the sheltered life I had been living. I knew that my community and my education were not enough for me to heal, and yet, there was always a part of me that wanted to bring back whatever I learned for my family, for my culture.

Even though it may seem impossible, while I raged at God, I also allowed God to guide and heal me—I actually demanded it. Some days I released all my anger and resentment until I was thoroughly exhausted. Only then could I make room for the healing and peace that my body craved, and I let God fill up the broken places.

When I allowed for all emotions to move through my body, over time I experienced a synthesis of mind, body, and spirit. I felt more room to become my true self. I made a point to nurture myself in ways that my soul needed, through creative means, through nature walks, through salt-water baths, through prayer. A spark within me began to brighten with each release. Hearing birds sing each morning was a sound of sweetness that fed me, along with the sun on my face, and the softness of orange hibiscus flowers that opened for me. I slowly came back to life.

Carol Sydney writes

Once you begin experiencing the magic of life and start recognizing *the miracles that are occurring in your life every day, you are ready to begin encountering your true essence . . . you will feel an acceleration of your body's wellness and the remaining fear your cells are holding will be thrown off . . . Remember, as with all letting-go, when fear leaves your body, grief is felt and you rise in vibration and joy.*[47]

A Touch

I wipe your face,
and in your sweat and pain,
I am tempted to stay in suffering—
yours and my own.

Yet I hear you call me,
beyond myself.
The moment I touch you,
you take me beyond this moment,
teaching me
that *all* fearful thoughts
tempt us,
attack our minds,
steal our spirit.

But you show me the way,
in the moment of that touch—
and all the earth stood still.

You walk beside me,
guiding me
through the dark waters
of my mind,
in the broken bones
of my body.

You promise *never* to leave me,
whenever I walk this walk,
for suffering is never
the end,
never the destination.

You offer me peace—
my birthright—
if I but touch your face,
and face each fear
with quiet calm.

Death, suffering,
can never stop
heaven on earth—
we must resurrect ourselves
to our true destiny,
beyond moments—
beyond roles we play—
beyond pain of illusion—
and beyond the tenderness
of my touch.

I know now
that I *can*
step into my resurrection.

Whenever I yearn to touch you,
I allow you to touch my soul—
and then I can claim
my true lineage:

For
I Am
Living Daughter
of my Living God.

Tina Karagulian

Whatever It Takes to Heal

Right after I received my social work degree and began to heal my abuse memories, my husband and I moved from Massachusetts to Texas. During the course of my healing, I enrolled in a class that promised to introduce its students to many different healing techniques. While experiencing a hands-on-healing technique, I found that heat automatically began to emanate from my hands; I later discovered that it would soothe my body each time I relived a terrible memory. Body memories always require tending to the body—releasing memories did not feel so overwhelming when combined with massage, baths, and healing energy through my hands. Each time I put my hands on my heart, I felt a divine presence guide my healing, so that I did not feel so alone, and so that I could be freed.

I called upon Christ, and I also called upon Archangel Raphael—the archangel of healing—to clear my body of a thick, toxic energy. I noticed that when I called upon them, I could feel healing passing through my hands. I knew that I was not doing the healing, but that it came from God. It was such a blessing to feel Raphael and Christ with me. What a difference! It brought me great comfort when I felt so alone.

During this time, I also enrolled in a class taught by Gina Lalli on *Patanjali's Yoga Sutras,* a sacred text from India; Gina taught from Rammurti S. Mishra's translation of the *Yoga Sutras, The Textbook of Yoga Psychology.* [48] I know I was led to feed the hunger for knowledge within me, to help me put words to the spiritual truths that I have intuitively felt all my life. In our weekly classes, we first chanted the lesson in Sanskrit, and then learned the meaning of how to apply it in our lives. The chanting sounded very similar to Armenian, and I felt the impact of ancient sounds resonating within me. Gina explained that

One could write a paragraph in an attempt to capture the real meaning of a single four letter word in Sanskrit. It is best if one can get the general meaning of a word, the concept that it represents, in the English exposition of it and then to keep repeating the Sanskrit word, not a

translation of it, as you encounter it when reading the text. Sanskrit words have a power all their own and may reveal more meaning as you contemplate them.[49]

Later I learned that the Aum is similar to Amen, and when chanting either word, you call the Holy Spirit within you to guide you.[50] Yet the Sanskrit Aum seemed to create a deeper imprint upon my body. I found that it helped release those body memories and reconnect me to my soul. Yahaira Volpe writes that Aum

. . . aligns the four bodies, the physical, emotional, mental and spiritual . . . Notice that the vibration creates a calming peace inwardly and outwardly so it affects also those close to you . . . it is the universal sound of GOD the creator the Source of all life.[51]

The combination of healing energy through my hands and chanting with my voice would shift painful energy and emotions from my body, helping to heal my painful memories. In the yoga sutra lessons, I became aware of the presence of wisdom guiding me, too. I compared inner child work I learned from Western psychology with the wisdom of Patanjali, and they overlapped. I learned about Patanjali's steps to develop the ability to watch ourselves, to detach from our thoughts and senses so that we can connect with God, freeing us from the suffering we identify with.

Likewise, in my inner child work, I was learning to detach from the emotional pain of a memory so that I could see myself as someone who *had* the experience, instead of believing that I was *one* with the experience, forever embedded in it. During these moments of detachment I would increase my connection to the present moment, to what is real— the constancy of God. By focusing on my breath, slowing it down, I allowed for healing to enter my body, and room to see the thoughts and beliefs attached to any suffering I experienced.

At the end of each yoga study class, we would meditate as a group. We sat with God in silence. It was the beginning of a formal practice of connecting with God regularly. After a year and a half, Gina began interpreting the *Bhagavad Gita (The Song of the Blessed Lord)*. She taught us this interpretation of Chapter 1:

Before you make big changes in your life, you have terrific doubts. You pull back energy you need to make that change. You feel it will fall apart, afraid it won't reform. It's chaos. Before having freedom, there's chaos. Yet change is inevitable: something in us or outside us can stir us to change, or a spiritual urge to get conscious. You must find your own right action, your own unique way. But you come up against resistance from your family, and from within. Yet you must give up something in order to create anew, in order to be free.[52]

Gina Lalli's description matched my experiences of healing from body memories, and also the spiritual awakenings I had had during many phases of my life. She writes

The very actions that bind us may be transformed into actions that free us . . . However, the Bhagavad Gita stresses more the individual's dharma, each man fulfilling in actions the potential of his temperament (if he is an artist, he will practice his art, etc.), being true to his own temperament, and not trying to emulate the potential of another. Each person has his own unique right action, called Sva-dharma (one's own right action) . . . You don't always know if you are taking the right action, but the intention is most important, that you sincerely wish it is the right action and that it is doing no harm and will, in fact, benefit the whole universe.[53]

I felt Christ guiding my every step, showing me the ways to free myself of pain, showing me what my unique right action would be in the world. I knew I was not an expert in these sacred texts; it is a lifelong journey to be so, but I was open to the spiritual truths that satisfied my thirst for the heart's wisdom. I began seeing a richness in other religions and spiritual practices, and that God was the center of it all. I put my experiences within a context, to learn to watch myself, to detach from the pain while I allowed myself to express it. Detachment was not denial that an event took place or limiting the expression of emotions; it was a shift in focus onto God—that which never changes. Some suffering is inevitable, and yet we can find ways to help us move through the suffering. Over time, painful events that are felt do not remain with us with the same emotional intensity. We become free of events and feelings that weigh us down, that keep us from peace.

I felt that God wanted me to continue to tie together what I was learning in my yoga study class when I came upon Paramahansa Yogananda's book *Autobiography of a Yogi*.[54] Yogananda believed that we can be freed through our direct experience of God. In his book, he refers to Christ throughout its pages, and again, I felt Christ's guiding hand showing me the way. Bible references filled the book, and I was shown in detail how we can live as disciples, how we can improve ourselves, how we can become like Christ. The unconditional love that Christ represents is here for everyone, and when we embrace it fully, we can choose to become more Christ-like, too. Jesus Christ embodied the unconditional love that resides within each one of us. When we each invite and ignite that highest form of love within us, we become one with it, and commune with it.

Yogananda explained that each of us has a unique temperament, and that we can use our natural temperaments to build our connections with God. Some of us express our path with devotion, or *bhakti*, some with a focus on wisdom, some with action. There are many ways to be with God, yet often there is one temperament that stands out for us, based upon who we are.

Gina Lalli described these various temperaments that can be enhanced through different yoga practices, found in the *Bhagavad Gita*:

Karma Yoga—*remaining in touch with the spiritual worlds while engaged in the actions of daily life.*
Jnana Yoga—*to have a direct experience of Spirit through refined discernment.*
Buddhi Yoga—*to see the Light of the Spirit everywhere, in every thing.*

Bhakti Yoga—*devoted attention and love toward the One Life present everywhere.*

These four yogas are considered to be inseparable . . . A seeker may begin with the one most suited to his individual temperament.[55]

Yogananda described himself as devotional, and since I was also devotional by nature, he gave me a blueprint of how I could increase my devotion with Christ as my teacher. But, then something surprising happened. I read Yogananda's multi-dimensional description of Divine Mother, and his devotion to *Her*:

The Divine Mother is that aspect of God which is active in creation . . . She is characterized by many names and many forms, according to the qualities She represents . . . Her upraised hand signifies universal blessing; the others hold, symbolically, prayer beads (devotion), pages of scripture (learning and wisdom), and a jar of holy water (purification).[56]

Many times he described how swift his prayers were answered when praying to Divine Mother. He would often meditate upon *Her* to guide him. Many Christian nuns refer to God as Mother, so the concept was not new to me. What I felt was that *She* was speaking to me through various traditions, calling forth devotion within me.

By sharing his own story, Paramahansa Yogananda also shows us the mistakes he made during his life, how he learned from them, and how he bridged the eastern and western worlds, showing the unity of spiritual traditions. I intuitively felt I had been groomed for a similar call. Like some Christian mystics, he taught the road of self-realization, or direct experience with your Creator, as the way to freedom. His life story helped me to learn to forgive myself and others, and to learn to develop my already devotional connection to both Jesus Christ and God as Mother.

As part of my expanded learning, I also began to read about Native American traditions that connect with Mother Earth. Through the shamanic practice of soul retrieval,[57] I learned that we can retrieve parts of our souls that are lost during trauma, yet another way for us to integrate when we are shattered. A few years later, I met Milo Beaver, a native healer who spoke to me about my work with others, telling me that people would come to me, and that I would offer a space of healing for them. He said that I might not know where they were headed, but that it would not matter. I would be led in the moment with each of them, even if for just one meeting. He confirmed my role as healer. And then he asked, over and over again,

What's stopping you?

I still had moments of doubt that held me back, moments of holding back my presence in the world. I felt I was not wise enough, not clear enough. Some of those old limiting beliefs that I carried would creep in. The words of Milo Beaver have stayed with me; I felt God speaking through him, encouraging me to claim my gifts, that I would be led the rest of the way. Many times we meet someone who gives us encouragement and affirmation to stay focused on our path.

Through the native traditions I was able to reclaim my connection to my intuition and Mother Earth. My deep connection to nature returned to me; I noticed that when I connected with Mother Earth, something changed within me. I learned a meditation in which I imagined roots of light descending from my feet into the core of the earth, and then swirling upward into my body. I felt grounded by the pulse of love coming from Mother Earth. She is more than the ground we walk upon— she *is* my Mother. When I connected to Mother Earth, any pain I felt with another would melt away. I could love anyone who had caused me harm, and, as long as I felt my connection to Mother Earth, I could forgive anyone anything. This was the first visceral awareness of how I could be centered in unconditional love, able to forgive freely.

I began to recall, years before, sitting in that tree at my elementary school, knowing that I was deeply loved. It all came back to me. I had cut off knowing about Mother Earth to survive in the world, but I had also prevented myself from feeling her love. I knew then that connecting to a Divine Mother was crucial to any type of healing. I began to see the lines of demarcation dissolving; the Divine Feminine is everywhere, takes many forms, and we can get all that we need if we look to our Creator in any way that feels the *most personal* for us. Father? Mother? Spirit? It matters only to us. These names are more than just markers— they are portals to a Source, the Creator behind and around us all.

For several reasons, the human part of me needed a Mother in all these forms to nurture me, to fill in the gaping holes. I learned that each time I experienced a body memory, each time I faced a fear by rebirthing an aspect of myself, when I called upon Her, I felt a swift transformation take place. She is my inner knowing.

To this day, I utilize everything I have learned on the journey to find *whatever it takes to heal*. It is that inner surrender to our own individual and wise knowing, in whatever form it takes. Does my body feel balanced, grounded, and aligned? If I feel discomfort or irritability, what truth do I need to express? Do I need to chant or sit in meditation in order to bring about balance for myself? Does this action I want to do express a balanced wisdom and love for myself and others? How can I articulate my needs clearly and accurately for myself and then express my words lovingly for others to hear? What am I doing that contributes to this imbalance? I allow the energy to pass through my hands and body, and I say the prayer, *Allow me to see and understand what is blind to my understanding.* These questions, in addition to the wisdom of various faith traditions I learned during this time of my life, continue to teach me to heal, balance, and receive wisdom.

Love is an attempt to change a piece of a dream-world into reality.

Henry David Thoreau

Dream of Pomegranates

Twenty years after the first body memory that began my initiation into healing, I had a dream about my paternal grandfather. Even though I had long forgiven him and did not have the emotional intensity of the memories anymore, there were a few pieces of closure that wanted to take place. In the dream, I was in a simple building out in the middle of the country, trying to work, but unable to do so. I saw people I did not completely trust. They were not frightening to me, but I had to watch them. I had to get past the ice we were all walking on to go to the other side. The ice was indoors. I saw a man slipping as he walked with his shoes on the ice, so I immediately lay down on my belly, into penguin mode, sliding with my torso as if I had done this my entire life.

I got to the other side safely without falling down or breaking any part of my body.

I saw many people looking at me. I then heard the name *Simee-ohn* or *Simon*.

My paternal grandfather's name was Simon. Simon Karagulian. I saw him as the man he once was, then I saw the evil that was all around him, coming through him as it did when he was on Earth. I asked Divine Mother and Christ to be behind me, and they said they were. I asked very calmly for Archangel Michael to take away the darkness around my grandfather, for the taunting voices did not have their power over me anymore. Michael did, and then I saw that my grandfather wanted to talk to me.

I calmly said to him,

I forgive you, but I want to know something: can you see what you did to us on Earth? What are you going to do to make it right somehow?

I thought of how he hit my grandmother daily until there was nothing left of her soul, not to mention the acts of violence he had done to me and my sister. I was calling for amends for us all, a way to put things right. I knew the importance of speaking truth as a form of outward action. Each act of truth creates an opening, a possibility for a better outcome.

He had collected a bunch of what looked like pomegranate seeds, saying they were rubies. They were hard gemstones that shone. I saw a flat basket of these gems in his arms, and he motioned for me to take them.

As I looked at the basket, I realized it did not represent financial abundance, but all the parts of our souls that he took away from each and every one of us, any person who needed healing. It was then that I saw my paternal grandmother, Isgouhi, come to me. I called to her, *Mama!* She looked at me with such clarity, something she could not do on Earth. She locked her eyes with mine. She looked fabulous, shining and strong, so different from the lost and feeble woman I remembered as a child. They said she was senile, but I knew there was so much more to her story, even then. She had weathered such physical abuse from her husband, but right now she looked at me in her true form. She said to me, *How I love you!* Then she grabbed the ruby pomegranates, and began pouring them over my head, over and over again, until I felt refreshed. She said she had been waiting to do this for many years, always wishing she could have given me so much more than she could when she was alive on earth. I said that I wanted anyone who felt lost to feel this, too, to be showered with pomegranates, seeds of the hearts of all grandmothers. She said that all *will* be restored, that I could count on that.

Something began to shift inside me. I often hold things in my body until I can speak truth to the ones who need to hear it. There were many times when I have been impatiently waiting for a point of release, to see certain changes in my own lifetime. My family's healing has been one of them.

Isgouhi fastened her pearl necklace around my neck. It looked just like the one I had found in her pocketbook when she died, and I took it as a remembrance of her. I was only eight years old then. Over the years, I had lost the necklace; yet, it did not matter now, for she was putting one on my neck that would never be lost or taken. It represented her love for me, and it was around my throat, around my voice. I hugged her for such a long time. What a difference it was to have her fully restored before me!

I turned back to my grandfather and said,

I release you and send you blessings.

I picked up a handful of the ruby pomegranate seeds and placed them in my pockets. The rest I saw were taken to all those who needed them, all those in my family line for generations back, and anyone else in the world who needed them. It was a form of soul retrieval, much like those done by shamans all over the world. I knew that Armenians and Turks alike could also receive the same kind of healing, too—a healing that begins with willingness.

I knew that the slippery ice of places inside me did not deaden my soul. I felt love swirling all around me, and knew that sometimes we hold onto things until we have the right time and place to release them, that there is no judgment or expectation that it be done sooner than the right time. Something deep inside me knew that I had to do it this way, and created the scenario where I could speak my truth. I felt so grateful. Something definitely was made right in that dream vision.

When I woke, I wondered about the meaning of penguins and pomegranates. I felt the penguin to mean that I would have the ability to stomach any icy patch to get to the other side, that no more falling or injury would take place. I would be able to maneuver in places that were once slippery, and I could also have some fun while I maneuvered!

The ruby pomegranate seeds represent rootedness, continuity of life, and a restoration of the feminine strength. Armenians have a strong connection to pomegranates, for they were grown in the old country. They were hard as stone in my dream, and I believe that to mean that they cannot perish. They reminded me, too, of the pomegranate seeds that tied Persephone to the Underworld, to Hades, but now, I felt that my grandfather, who had lived a life of Hell, was returning the pomegranates to me, taking away the thing that bound us and trapped us all. He was releasing his hold. He gave back pieces of our collective heart.

The Annunciation of My Soul

Meeting of two wondrous beings!
You, oh messenger of light,
swift on wing,
you sought out
the physical incarnation of the
Divine Feminine Mother God,
who long ago
chose Mary as her vessel,
to birth Unconditional Love
in a new way—
for Divine Mother
is the Ultimate Creator,
the Holy Spirit that whispered
through your words, Gabriel,
planted a seed in you, Mary,
and was birthed in you, Christ.
May she speak, plant, and birth
Her unending love
within the depths of my soul.[58]

Tina Karagulian

Motherhood: Birthing Voice and Child

A very strong calling that was stirring within me was the call to become a mother. I longed to pass on wisdom to my child, to bring a love and healing to a new generation. I had to bring everything I was to this passionate dream—I could not hold back all that I was integrating, and I made a great effort to verbalize what I needed in my marriage. It was a painful time, because I believed that when I made a marriage vow, a sacrament, it would be forever. I prayed that we could move forward together, for I knew that anything was possible with God. Yet I had buried something deep within me for quite some time, and there was no way for it to come forth. While wanting to birth something deep within me, I wanted to bring forth a child, too; the burial that took place within me gave room for neither.

I questioned the call to make room for my soul over and over again, wondering if it were from God or just a temptation from the world. I remembered what I learned from *The Bhagavad Gita*, that the chaos was building for something else to be created within me. My body spoke up to clarify the matter for me, when nothing else could. I knew that an illness in the body can mean many different things, depending on the person and situation. For some, it is a vehicle to break ourselves and others open to a deeper love. For others, it is our bodies telling us that something is wrong and needs attention and a new direction—changes that can bring about pain for others, but also changes that can heal. For some, it is all of the above.

I thought of Mother Mary, birthing an important part of herself, even when others did not understand her. She is a model for women who surrender to a divine call inside them. I found myself grieving a lot during that time. My mother sent me a pair of earrings for my birthday made by my artist cousin Talin. On each earring she painted a very tiny image she called a saint. Each had a halo, the color of gold and red, and a man with dark hair and beard. What I saw were priests that looked like they were from an Orthodox tradition, like the Armenian Apostolic Church. I realized again how much the priesthood meant to me, and I began to wear the earrings as if they were my vestments. They were symbols of my spiritual voice needing a place in the world.

At the time, the Armenian Church community in Texas held its services at an Orthodox Church downtown, since the Armenian Church community did not have a church building of its own. On one occasion, as we prepared for the service, the visiting priest walked into the altar area, preparing the chalice and the wine. An Armenian woman from our community went up to ask the priest what else he would need, when a man, the sexton of the church, came rushing down the aisle to them, dragging his upright vacuum cleaner with him. He had been vacuuming the church during our arrival. He berated the woman for stepping into the altar area, speaking with strong words that women were not allowed in that sacred space. I knew what was behind his words: the belief that women were unclean, that they were not holy—that women who menstruate should not receive communion, let alone be in an altar space. The woman from our community retreated, but all I could focus on was the vacuum cleaner. There was an inanimate object standing at attention *on* the same altar space where this woman was not permitted. The painful irony before me was that the symbol of something that makes things clean was contrasted with the woman who is seen as unclean—yet women cannot be vacuumed up. The deep sadness inside me returned, calling forth my own feelings of being unappreciated and dishonored; I yearned, too, to stand on holy ground, in sacred spaces, a woman as worthy as any man.

That Easter I did not want to attend the Armenian Church service; I did not want to sing when I could not be fully accepted, fully included in the church. I heard Christ call to me, saying,

Just sing for me, as if we are the only ones in the room.

He was calling me to the communion that we shared whether we were in church or not. That communion has been constant throughout my life. As I focused on him, I smiled. He opened my heart to a love that has always sustained me when nothing else could. That day, I was part of a four-person choir, and I sang my heart out. People came up to us afterward and kept remarking on how beautiful the music was that day, especially with only four people singing. I have often heard that, when I sing in small choirs: a deeper sound fills the room. I have said that it is because angels have chimed in with us. When we focus our hearts as much as we can, amazing openings are created and miracles occur.

Although I felt a spiritual presence that day, in the midst of great pain, I could not shake that I had to make a change for my soul. I longed to share the many levels of my soul in every area of my life, and to have those levels tended and reciprocated. Women often know in their guts when things are not right, but to put words to the inner process may initially be difficult. Emotions and vulnerability take center stage and must be weeded through. Yet when a partner chooses to listen deeply to the inner voice of a loved one, there is a marriage of souls, again and again.

Sometimes poets and mystics have a language that is unique, yet in the deeper listening, the words begin to make sense. When a woman attempts to find words for wordless places within her and is not heard by her partner, something shatters inside. She must find her own words and continue to find ways to bring forth what her soul is telling her.

Clarissa Pinkola Estés writes that when a woman's mate continues to strive to understand and to connect with her, they both shine for one another.[59]

If we hold back or try to hide our soul's purpose, it will push to come through in symbols and dreams until it is heard. The task for a partner and her mate is to look deeply at the dreams and symbols, finding a common language to describe that process, and trusting in the journey with one another. It means choosing love that goes beyond words, beyond what society may deem as the only way. A willingness to listen in this way to the soul of the other will always yield lasting results. A partner's role is to listen and support the soul of the other, for both are nurturers of each other's calling.

I repeatedly shared the language of my soul, but it did not make sense to those around me. I longed for a community who already knew the language of my soul. I wanted my eyes to shine. When January rolled around, it was time for a New Year's resolution. A force came out of me that I could not contain. I said aloud, more to myself than to anyone else:

I will not compartmentalize my life anymore.

I did not want to live a partitioned existence anymore. My compartmentalization began at an early age. I felt the urge to bring things back together. I would no longer hide the healing journey I had embarked upon, or my spiritual call.

My body was crying out and I needed to listen to it. I knew that if I divorced, I might never marry anyone again, nor have the opportunity to have a child. I knew that in my culture I was going to go up against intense opposition. I knew that members of my family and the Armenian community would not understand my decision. I went into nature, into a greenbelt canyon, and asked God what I should do. I felt the healing presence of Mother Earth all around me as I bared my soul before God.

New Skin

At times we wear the skins of
caretaker, tender listener, and
supporter of others' dreams and visions—
so that they may thrive on their intended roads.

At times we walk alongside
the death and suffering of others,
so that they may not feel alone,
so that love's true essence may revive and resurrect.

Yet when we courageously enter the darkness
of our deepest fears and unanswered dreams—
then the true alchemy begins:

With new eyes we see the needs and wants
that clamor for our attention,
and begin to let go
of unnecessary obligations.

We learn to quiet all the voices that tempt
and taunt us from inner peace,
releasing the hold they have
within our bodies and minds.

We walk steadfastly into our center,
allowing for the One True Voice
to emerge and guide,
daily surrendering to Her wisdom.

We listen inside voiceless places of our heart,
until the silence spurs us into action
that feeds our deepest reserves.

We feel the vulnerability of new skin,
yet allow its sleekness to breathe us.

For our every weakness
we receive increasing compassion
that naturally ripples out
and envelopes others.

Each time we focus our attention
on *our* soul's vision,
the warrior within stands tall,
protecting a newly emerging creativity
that is initially unrecognizable,
peacefully familiar,
yet strongly resolute.

Once we claim the wild voice of our soul,
there's no turning back.

Tina Karagulian

Ask and You Will Receive[60]

I was definitely asking. The first answer I received was to speak with a colleague at the counseling agency where I worked. For the one and a half years since I'd met Pat, I'd felt a strong connection with him, and I trusted his advice. Something about him made me feel so comfortable, as if I knew him from long ago. When I walked in nature and prayed, I felt a loving presence encourage me to speak with him. I believed that he would assist me in overcoming any obstacles within me.

I knew that this pull toward him was my soul calling me. It was not desire run amok, but a movement toward something that would feed both our souls' purpose. I had this sense that I could truly love this man in a deep way, somehow knowing that he could see the many levels of the inner me and I him in a way that neither of us felt before. I never knew anything about his personal life. I prayed and prayed about it, for it to be released from me. I prayed for God to give me clarity, so that the highest good might happen for everyone involved. I did not want to cause undue harm to anyone. What I heard was this:

If Pat chooses to be with you, it would be blessed. Yet if he does not make that choice, do not worry. God will guide your next step.

I experienced a peace in my body, an ability to feel alive and centered. I knew that I did not have any feelings of guilt or regret about moving forward with my life. It was up to God and also up to Pat if we were to be together. I asked for the highest good *for all*. From my experience of prayer, I knew I had to let go of the outcome completely. A peace filled me that I knew had to be from God, for I felt that whatever the outcome would truly be fine. I would be led. I thanked God for that answer, and felt that I somehow passed a test, that I was not acting just from a place of desire.

Years later I heard Dr. Luke Timothy Johnson[61] share in his own story that sometimes God's call can be messy, that at times those around us can be hurt. He was a Benedictine monk when he met his wife, who was already married with six children. He said that following our call, learning and healing sometimes take many years before we can see our lives come full circle. In the human moment, it is often hard to see that perspective. I was about to embark upon that same sort of messy call, another time in the desert.

Pat decided to take the journey with me, and within three weeks, we changed the course of our lives, leaving behind marriages, houses, and money. Through the process, we lost our counseling jobs. We lost many friends and supports as well. Some in our inner circle judged us very harshly. Very few understood this journey we were on; since I was adept at reading people's thoughts, I could intuit that many thought it was just a passing fling, an error in judgment. The human part of me felt enormous emotional pain in losing the relationships I had cared about. As a counselor, I knew that just one major life change, positive or negative, can have an extraordinary impact on someone's life. Between the two of us, we made five of those life changes within one year.

I was led to leave the Armenian Church community, so that I could make room for a deeper call. At that point in time, leaving the Armenian Church was the most difficult attachment I had to give up, since so many of my inner spiritual experiences were interwoven with its liturgical expressiveness. Because there were few Armenian communities, I knew I would have to do without my beloved church service. I called Der Arnak, not only as a priest, but also as a family friend; I asked him to give me communion when he arrived for his next visit to Texas. I told him what was happening in my life, and said that I needed a quiet location to meet with him. Given his history of breaking rules in support of women in the church, I assumed that he would understand my desire to follow that calling now, the desire to get back on track with my discernment. He promised he would give me communion when he came to Texas, but when he came to see me, he said he had never intended to give me communion. I knew that he judged the outer appearances of such a change in my life without understanding my inner process. My words of explanation were useless, my inner call dismissed. That moment was probably the worst moment of all—a cherished symbol of my connection to Christ withheld from me. Driving away, I was devastated.

As I drove away, I saw what was quite unusual during the daylight hours. A bright orange fox ran across the road before me. I had never seen one up close before, and its beauty filled me. I was given this beautiful gift, so I would know that I was moving toward something.

Later when I spoke with my mother about the incident, she said that she'd had a conversation with Der Arnak. She asked him why he had refused me communion, and he said that, given the circumstances and his vow as a priest, he would not give me communion. I had expected her to fight harder for me, yet the only thing she said was that she understood his position. Years later, I came to understand that given the context of her generation, her speaking up at all was a huge leap. But in that moment, I was broken-hearted. I really needed them both to hear me.

With the loss of my Armenian community, I felt bereft. Yet my dear friend and poet Diana Der-Hovanessian[62] reminded me that she was still there, rallying behind me, an Armenian woman and sister through it all. She encouraged my writing, and she encouraged my soul to shine. She was the bedrock I needed back then.

She was not the only one. The night when I was denied communion, I felt my maternal grandmother around me and heard her loud and clear. Even though some members of my family did not understand or support my decision to be with Pat, she made a point to say to me,

Don't worry about what others can't see; you picked the right one! I will always watch over you.

I felt her embrace me within my heart, and that held me for a very long time.

If you can't embrace being vulnerable, pray "I want to be vulnerable about being vulnerable." If you can't stand the fact of your own weakness, pray "I need to be weak enough to say that I am weak." If you hesitate to name your sadness, let that come to speech: "I need to tell You I am sad." . . . Vulnerability is a fruit for which we need to acquire a taste.

Mary C. Earle[63]

Go confidently in the direction of your dream! Live the life you've imagined . . . [64]

Henry David Thoreau

Walden

The most incredible gift through all the upheaval was that I was pregnant with the child I always wanted! What a gift! His presence pulsed within my heart, and I felt his amazing soul grow within me, drinking deeply from his parents' love. I had the authentic life I always hoped to live, and I did not have to hide any part of myself anymore. I could pass along my knowledge, wisdom, and love without censorship, without hesitation. Pat and I intended to give our son all that we knew: our time, our poetry, our wisdom, and our hearts.

I had a job teaching UNIX operating system classes at Motorola, a job I loved. Teaching allowed me the opportunity to pass along knowledge, and also to be a ham for my adult students. I found that through my use of humor and the connections it forged with my students, the class material was more easily transmitted and retained.

Yet one day, when I was six months pregnant, while swimming in a local pool, I heard very clearly,

You are going to lose your job with Motorola, but don't worry; some day all will be restored to you.

Sure enough, the next day, my employer called to say that all the Motorola contract instructors were let go. Now we had no income at all. The restoration, the *some* day, would take many more years to come, many years of getting very clear and releasing all that was not necessary. We began our desert time as a couple. Stripped of so much, I felt like Job in the Bible, in constant communication with God, amidst all that was taken away. We were streamlining our lives, starting again from the ground up.

We embarked upon our vagabond days—in search of home and new livelihoods. We were grateful that Pat's parents took us in for a few months as we got settled. It was very difficult for us, yet I felt that bringing up Walden was my first priority. How beautiful was this baby I had! He was very aware, very in tune, and I was convinced that he wanted both his mother and father around as much as possible. Not easy to do when you had to live in the world and secure income. Through this humbling period, I got very focused on him.

Pat finally found a full-time job to sustain us. There were many days when I was exhausted, trying to carve a new life and create stability for us all. Invariably, the days I really looked forward to nap when Walden napped were the days when he wouldn't sleep! Thank goodness for PBS and *Mr. Rogers' Neighborhood*!

Walden was bright-eyed since his birth, aware of sounds and images all around him. He and I would lie in the backyard and look up at the tall pine trees, following the squirrels as they scampered back and forth. I taught him *Itsy Bitsy Spider* with a jazz beat, while Pat and I often sang rock and roll and pop songs as lullabies. I also sang my beloved church hymns and the Armenian lullaby *Oror Im Balas*[65] to help him sleep. Walden would eat pesto by the spoonful without flinching, as he soaked up the world around him. We drew pictures together and created buildings out of building blocks.

Understandably, I was overprotective of my baby, not letting just anyone watch him. I was wary because of my own childhood; I had to make sure that this next generation was able to start anew, with instincts intact. There were times I railed against Mother Mary, saying I could use her to come by and babysit more than once in a while. I longed for more of a connection to other women, who would help me raise Walden in the same tender way I envisioned. I was looking for my tribe.

I knew I was sensitive, but I found that during my motherhood phase, my sensitivity went off the charts. I breastfed my son for two years, and felt my entire focus was upon creating a safe and loving environment in which he could grow. The tall pine trees in our backyard gave me strength and filled my lungs with sweetness. It was an important nesting time for me, and I felt the incredible need to stay in a protective bubble, to nurture this new life, and give Walden all that he needed to thrive. I never went to malls, or to crowded places, but took daily walks with Walden around the reservoir, feeling the breeze off the water filling us both.

Throughout my entire life, but particularly during this phase of my life, I experienced visitations from people in spirit, people who had died, but were trapped in the earth plane. Somehow, they knew that I could communicate with them. I often said to Pat that I was a counselor on both sides of the veil, for those on earth, and for those who passed on. At times, I have had glimpses of a time before this incarnation, when I assisted others who had died and needed a safe haven to sort through the life they had just lived. During this sensitive time in my life as a new mother, I found myself much more open to hearing the needs of others, even those in spirit form. I often felt their presence and heard what they needed, yet did not see them. One day, however, when Walden was playing in another room, I actually saw something as well. Someone was showing me the manner of his death, that he had been suffering from some sort of trauma, unable to be free of it. I felt strongly that he was a Native American who had been massacred near the location of the manmade reservoir near us, but it was long ago, when white settlers first entered the area. There are times that those who die tragically become disoriented, unable to see angels guiding them, but they can see humans who are sensitive to their presence. During these types of encounters, I call upon Archangel Michael and Archangel Raphael, the protecting and healing archangels, to assist me. I tell these lost souls, and anyone else who is with them, to go with my two friends, to trust their guidance. I send my own blessings, and invariably, the room is filled with peace once again. I know that they are free at last. This type of service never disturbs me, for my guidance is often heeded—it is an opportunity to serve others, and I do so willingly.

However, I continued to encounter *people* on Earth who did *not* see or hear me, who did not honor the gifts I had to offer; when I tried in vain to communicate with them, I did not seem to make an impact. During this particularly sensitive period of time in my life, I was deeply in tune with an internal barometer, and any type of dissonance with the outside world felt like too much. If I heard a lot of negativity from someone, I did not want Walden around that person. If someone was not aware of his or her negativity, then I could not ensure that it would be censored in front of my son. I felt that I had to protect my child over all others, to give him a chance to grow and thrive. There were family members who were unaware of the painful words they used, and the words felt like verbal attacks. On a human level, I had to make a choice for life for me and my son. Only those who have lived a painful history can understand how much suffering it creates to have to cut off communication with family. If there were another way to create that bridge, to heal that connection, I would have done so. I had to trust God to take over where my human self could not. I was faced with a very difficult decision—one that hurt me deeply. I prayed and prayed to God about how to proceed. In the end, I felt I had no other choice. I made a point of saying to God,

I need to do this right now, but if at any time you feel I need to make contact again, I will do so.

Intuitively, I knew that for me to emerge whole, I needed to continue to protect whatever was sacred within me, so that I could be the best mother I could for my child.

There are times when you are stripped down and must tend to only that which is necessary for your own nurture.

I had been a caretaker for others my entire life, yet no one taught me how to create boundaries that would nurture the new life within me (my soul life and my physical child, too). I knew that if I did not listen to my inner guidance, I would be lost. Yet I longed for the possibility that reconciliation might take place. I felt both sides of the pain viscerally, but I had to follow the inner call that was guiding me. To this day, I still honor that decision. Yet there is no doubt that on a deep personal level, it also brought great suffering to many others and me. Ultimately, I believe it was a call for all of our injured instincts to find a way to heal, each of us needing time to find that path of self-care.

In her memoir *The Knock at the Door,* Margaret Ajemian Ahnert describes how the terror of her mother's experiences during the Armenian Genocide passes through her own body, as if the invisible umbilical cord were still pumping from mother to child—not nutrients, but instead, heightened emotional fragments:

Sometimes I feel terror so acute, so delineated, the world closes in. Terror, like genes, gets passed down, from him to her, from you to me. I looked at Sara. What would she inherit? She was still holding my hand. I pulled away. I did it, understand, out of love. I did it to keep her safe.[66]

As mothers, our wombs and breasts represent life at such a primal level that giving to another can awaken the same memories that our mothers and grandmothers experienced during the same time in their lives. I needed time to sift through experiences, so that I would not unconsciously pass anything down to my son. It was something I knew I had to understand and to express, to pray about, but I wanted to be very conscious about what he was given. It has been important for me to name the ways I have instinctively moved to heal these broken places.

Clarissa Pinkola Estés explains the importance of solitude in discovering what is important in our lives.[67] Some women need quiet to clarify their inner voice, to know what is necessary not only for ourselves, but also for our children. If we do not allow for enough time for ourselves, if we allow only other people's needs to crowd our inner spaces, then we will not know how to receive our divine birthright. Without knowing how to fully receive, we cannot give others the same fullness.

At different times in my life, I have needed solitude, to focus on my inner process. As a mother, I still was very present for my son, teaching him skills that I had learned along the way. Yet I also had to carve out time to replenish myself. For women who have not seen others model that behavior, it means learning a new skill. Distraction from that focus would have hampered my ability to nurture at all. I had to recover the instinct for self-care as a model for my son.

Carol S. Pearson reminds us that the crucial tending of our souls is the same tending that a mother gives her unborn child.[68]

The most painful part of my journey has been not being able to tend to that inner process while also being emotionally available for my mother and my sisters. However, each time I judge myself for my need of solace and retreat, I allow unnecessary suffering to enter my heart. If I move into a space of allowing for us all to have our individual experiences, I know instead the deeper truth: that my heart has loved deeply, and I have wanted healing and reconciliation for us all. I had to trust that deeper soul truth and trust it to lead the way. I recently shared this emotional Catch-22 place with another Armenian—the feeling that we can never really enjoy ourselves or move forward because we do not want to leave anyone behind. That has been my journey, holding an invisible thread leading back to my mother, my sisters, my grandmother. I have felt a longing to bring fire to my family—something to warm their souls— joining with the fires they, too, have received.

Yet we must allow ourselves the time and readiness to receive our fire. We must love each other enough to give room to love and trust our different processes. If we cannot always be there for each other, we can pray with confidence that we will be reunited someday, whether in this world or the next. Sometimes we are to step out of the way for others to find their way. I prayed to God, trusting that all of us would have whatever we needed the minute we asked for it. I had to trust that larger perspective.

It still broke my heart. I have both the wisdom of seeing when to take care of myself and also the sensitivity to cry at times for the suffering of others. I held the vision of the day when we women could share our pomegranate rubies of tender self-care with each other, the fruits of our individual journeys. The gift is that after all these years, with time and awareness, I have been blessed to see a transformation take place for the women in my family line. It has meant listening to the nuances of each other's spirits, to notice what is alike and what is unique about us— listening with ears *and* hearts. It is choosing to refrain from judgment and harsh words, bringing awareness to what triggers us, and bringing out the goodness in one another. It means gently guiding one another to remember the blessings and strengths within each of us. In the end, each time a woman reaches the other side, she can offer her nurturing gems to another woman who is recovering her injured instincts. It is a shared offering—a celebration of the collective wisdom. But in the meantime, I had to be patient and keep listening to the voice within me.

My Heart is Full

And you, daughters of my soul,
have no fear[*]—
authentic self,
babe in new skin,
transparent heart,
wrapped in curvatures of hills,
held in the crooks of your valleys,
from Zeitun to where my heart lives,
there is no distance: **seerdus letzoon eh**. [**]
I walk with women who know this terrain,
who turn back and beckon me
across the threshold.
Mother of My Soil,
you call me inside the beat of drums
to bridge my inner worlds.
Now no one place is more real.
I plant my roots inside your bosom,
ever complete.[69]

Tina Karagulian

[*]Reference to the Bible passage from Ruth 3:11
[**]Armenian translation of *my heart is full*.

Reconciliation

On Palm Sunday in 2006, we joined an Episcopal church—it gave the three of us the spiritual community we needed. It was no accident that the word *Reconciliation* was part of the church's name. God led us there, and it was a perfect fit. Our community embraced us. My son experienced a church community, much as I had in Philadelphia, that saw him grow and enjoyed his answers during the children's sermons. I began to sing in the choir again. How I had missed singing all those years! Initially, it took getting used to singing hymns that I never knew before. They were not the Armenian hymns that were etched in my soul's DNA, but I came to love the new devotional hymns, too. I was shown that I loved singing to God, no matter the language. It was a healing time.

Our church has a tradition in which lay people can share their stories through a presentation or sermon. A good friend encouraged me to deliver a presentation about my story as an Armenian, about the genocide. I initially balked at the idea. How to cover such a topic? I knew that I would feel intense emotions around my grandmother's story, and that they would bring pain to my body. Yet, the idea of giving a sermon touched my spirit in such a beautiful way; here was also my chance to share how God strengthened both my grandmother's life and my own. I spent nine months—*yes, nine months*—writing that sermon.[70] I wrote it and rewrote it. I wrote part of my history, shared a bit of my grandmother's forced march through the desert and mixed it with my own, sharing how God was always there somehow, and the amazing people along the way.

A treasured memory of that church service was when my church choir sang my favorite Armenian hymn, *Soorp, Soorp (Holy, Holy)*:[71]

Holy, holy, holy Lord of hosts;
Heaven and earth are full of your glory.
Blessing in the highest.

Blessed are you who did come and are to come in the name of the Lord. Hosanna in the highest.

Soorp, Soorp is a hymn that always touches me to my core. Those angels and archangels are always getting in on the action! As I wrote my sermon, I connected very much with my maternal grandmother. One day, I got an incredibly painful sunburn. I had never gotten such a burn before. Knowing that my grandmother had walked through the desert, Walden said,

Mom, she probably got sunburned then.

Baffling as it may be, I never linked the two until his comment. Somehow, I was reliving a piece of her march. I felt her story searing through my skin, and I felt her suffering. I realized how many times she and my mother had not had time to heal from all they had suffered, how they were just expected to survive, work, cook, and keep going at all costs. I thought of my mother, of her sacrifices to come to a new country, to build a new life, too, initially without her parents around her.

While writing the sermon, I also spoke and corresponded with the Turkish author Taner Akçam,[72] whose books and lectures acknowledging the Armenian Genocide and whose attempts at reconciliation between Armenians and Turks at times brought about death threats and criticisms from some of his own Turkish people. He has healed many Armenians because of his willingness to speak the truth, and his dialogue with me created further healing and reconciliation in my own heart.

It was around the time of the sermon that I heard a voice, loud and clear, telling me,

You are strong enough to call your mother now, if you choose.

When I made the painful decision to withdraw from my family, I also made a request of God—to tell me when I was ready to take a step toward forgiveness and reconciliation. I did not believe I was ready or worthy. I shared what I heard with a friend who gently pointed out that what I heard was not a command, but a *choice*. I relaxed, knowing that we always have the option to choose out of our free will. Since God saw that I was ready, saw a strength in me I did not know I had, I knew that I could take that step. I had already been praying a lot to God, saying,

I don't know how to do this, but I ask you to open my heart.

Another dear friend *just happened* to share how she was able to bridge a similar gap in her family history, showing me the way. Sometimes a frozen moment from our past needs to be jostled awake, so that we can resume our lives. I knew that anything was possible, with God's help. I called my mother on her birthday. I began to reconcile with her, step by step. From then on, I always called her whenever it moved my heart to do so, never forcing anything, which made such a big difference. I was learning to act out of love and not obligation. I could see that she was trying to watch her words, to be kind, and that meant a lot to me. There were many times I felt an incredible warm rush of energy flow through me when I spoke to her, and I came to realize that so much pain and suffering were being healed for both of us. I knew that our prayers for one another through the years brought us to this moment. Healing was happening for the entire family—what a gift from God.

Bending Into

Do I dare say yes
to the One who waits upon
my every whisper?

Do I dare say yes
to the Holy Kiss
and breath
that scatter all doubt?

Do I dare say yes
as I stand upon
my inner cliffs of longing?

Do I dare walk into
unknown waters
with my Living God?

Do I dare rest
into the yes
of my own resurrection?

Tina Karagulian

*What is unfinished for you to experience? I had to die to know how much
I wanted to live. Not as in living longer, but as in living deeper, wider. As
a result of this one experience, those few moments of clock time, being
alive transformed from a train ride to a mountain bike adventure over
slick rock. But now I get to do the driving.*

Dawna Markova[73]

Mid-life Call: Coming Full Circle

Since I said the words,

God's will, not mine, be done,

all the remaining fears have come up to be healed, *along with* all the hidden callings. I keep revisiting the dream of the shadow man with his gun pointed at my heart, and I have had to make sense of the tornado inside of me.

Jean Springer, a spiritual director, encouraged me to find women with whom to meet regularly, to give additional support during this time of transformation. I tried again to create a *Side by Side* circle of women that would support this passage with me. Several dear women supported me, listening to my heart in the deepest way: D. Phelps, Dru Dunn, Aminah Ulmer, Xelena González, Lilas Harvey, Melanie Christenson, Terry Arata-Maiers, Rosalyn Falcon Collier, Kay Briggs, Perla Garcia, Betty Hart, and Jean Springer herself.

When I forgot to eat well or practice my yoga, I received help from my spirit sisters. They would take me out to eat, walk with me in nature, and help remind me how to stay connected to life. My love of color and art would also save me, to be the creative source when words were often hard to reach. I often found myself in stores just looking at colorful objects, holding them in my hand. I did not need to purchase them, but simply enjoyed the artistic inspiration behind them. When I did so, I felt connected to artists everywhere. Sometimes, I felt the urge to buy a postcard of bright flowers or a colorful wind chime. I took these objects home, until I was later inspired to make something bigger out of them. I painted the rooms of my home with the colors from many of the objects I found. As I painted each room of my house, I felt a similar shift take place in the rooms of my heart. As I began to ascend from my dark cave, everything took on more color and brightness. I was creating from a reconciled and internally integrated place, and it was very satisfying.

Daily prayer and rest have been the key to my midlife integration. There have been times that I could do nothing but give my body quiet time and sleep. Many times I felt the effect of Divine Mother's soothing hands over my anxious heart, and peace would come to me at a faster rate than ever before. Sometimes I felt cold, and it was beyond a physical cold. It was as if my spirit was shifting and needed time just to move energy. I would soak in a bath of sea salt and lavender essential oil drops, allowing my cold body to find its warmth again. I would rest afterward, then wake up refreshed. Other times, I would lie outside on the grass, allowing Mother Earth to nourish my transitions. If I rushed these transition times, I would get backlogged in some way. Time, nourishment, community, and creativity from my center were all that I needed.

Another internal shift that came with my midlife awakening is how to care for others. I had long been very committed to serving in the community and in my family, but I began to feel pulled to conserve my energies. I continued to do my loving part as wife and mother, and as a part-time therapist, but I did not feel compelled to give as much outside of those areas. I needed time to recalibrate, and it would guide the next phase of my life. Similarly, I needed time to recalibrate during my motherhood years as well, when my entire focus was on my son. It is another aspect of the detachment process that allows for a different way of relating with others. I now know that the detachment has allowed me to love with more of my soul. In midlife, the shift in how I serve and nurture others channeled its way through my writing and my speaking.

An essential part of this transformation was humor. It surrounded me, especially when I found that I was getting too lost, too serious, or too judgmental of myself. The dark places were melting away, revealing the goodness and silliness of life that were always there within me, but at times hidden. Dru Dunn gave me a white stone that had the word *giggle* on it. I put it in a place I could see every day. Dru's sharp wit and wisdom come through in teasing prods and uproarious giggles. It is always infectious, and I remembered just what a ham I really am—how easily I love to laugh. She reminded me that giggles were a real part of my soul, and it was time to exercise that muscle, too.

During my meditative conversations with Christ or Divine Mother, I would often hear wisdom spoken again and again, until they brought me back to my center. And just when I was becoming much too serious, I would also hear some silly or corny song lyric that shifted my mood instantly, cracking me up. To my surprise, I began to laugh out loud at certain serious stories from my past, making room for them to move to lightness. The goofy leather jacket of my dream reminds me that transformation also involves silliness. One Halloween, I dressed up as my very own superhero—Cheesy Humor Woman. I drew a slab of cheese on my shirt, bad puns on my back, and wore a cheesy yellow mask. Though my cheesiness does peek out at times, I have not given it enough room to come out and play. I have learned that laughing my way through a painful moment does not dishonor the experience, but shifts the intensity of it. I look forward to my humor's continued emergence during this next phase of my life.

I love to read books and watch movies that feed my soul, that tell stories of descent, integration, and reemergence through creativity. All the characters live within us, and when we love and appreciate all of them, especially the critical and judgmental ones, we are freed. The artist in me drank deeply from the well of transcendent imagery in the animated film *The Secret of Kells*,[74] in which the fairy/wolf-girl Aisling is the catalyst for a young boy's own creativity; as she sings a hauntingly beautiful song, I felt her calling out my own creativity. In a key moment, the boy Brendan must choose between his uncle's tyranny and his own creativity. Fused in my emotional response to the scene were the struggles of my own longings to be an Armenian priest, the collective Armenian experience of the terror and suffering in the Genocide, and the painful choices many of us make in moving forward into our deepest creativity.

The Secret of Kells and Hayao Miyazaki's film *Ponyo* both remind us that our seemingly dormant creativity can emerge once again in our lives, with more energy and focus. Seeing movie characters mirror parts of my own journey always reminds me that with every retreat into inner and outer silence, there can always be rebirth and integration.

During this transition time, I continued to learn new ways to bridge the integration within myself. I visited the Christ Healing Center,[75] where theophostic prayer is incorporated in their healing practices. Healers ask questions to help individuals go back into painful memories or times in their lives, but the focus of their work is not on human intervention: it is creating a space that allows Christ and us to have direct contact with each other. Healing takes place as entrenched beliefs shift; lies we have carried are brought to light and then healed. The healing practices mirrored my lifelong dialogue with Christ and God, and I was blessed to have the center's ministry reinforce my own connection. Rev. Jack Sheffield also blessed my emerging voice and my desire to preach and teach through a newly unfolding ministry.

Another form of integration during this time incorporated the concept of feeding that which needs feeding within us. Whatever part of us that needs healing, mothering, wisdom—a part of us that we may judge or reject or see as undeserving—is given acceptance or "food" from the integrated Self. We may also call upon an ally in Spirit to join us as we imagine dissolving our integrated self into food that is then fed to the needy or hungry parts of us. There is no more separation, and the process mirrors Jung's model of integrating aspects of ourselves. Lama Tsultrim Allione[76] offers a step-by-step process to do this in her book, and it reminds me very much of what we Christians do when we receive the spiritual food of communion.

By telling stories, by writing, I am also feeding the parts of me that have been mute for so long. Stories needed to be spoken, needed to be unearthed. During this midlife upheaval, I sat in meditation, apart from the world, but that was not enough. What deepened within me was my unique action, my way of expressing the divine. Words are part of my calling, to bridge people and experiences, to join them to their own stories. Chanting, singing, writing, and speaking are all ways to clear any heaviness I hold onto, and then I sit and wait to receive in stillness from a divine presence. For me, it is an integration of words and stillness. This is how I experience the weaving of the human and the divine within me—God is stitching me to *Her* bosom each time we connect in my heart. Yet, some of the remaining desires from my soul also needed expression. Some desires—once expressed—dissolved, while other desires only deepened. I had to pursue the thwarted call of the priesthood now, to push through whatever the young woman of my adolescence could not express thirty years ago.

. . . EVERY person is anointed by the Holy Spirit and becomes a potential minister in any given setting. This is what real unity is in the Body of Christ.

Jack Sheffield[77]

Mother's Day Sermon

I actively pursued the priesthood call, and I felt a desire to prepare and give a Mother's Day sermon[78] at my church—The Episcopal Church of Reconciliation. I prayed about it with Divine Mother, wondering if this pull inside me was to make room and support another woman to do the sermon, or if it was for me to give the sermon myself. In the end, I let go of the outcome, but simply expressed the desire. It kept coming back again and again: a green light within me to offer it myself. I wanted to give back to the incredible women of my church community—women who were the backbone, whose strength and wisdom filled the air, and yet who often enough did not receive enough recognition. The priests of my church gave me the green light.

I prepared a sermon and Prayers of the People section for the day's liturgy, and chose hymns that honored women. As I spoke, I felt a loving energy fill me, and I knew it came from Divine Mother. There was a beautiful strength in my voice that filled me up, and I saw it fill the congregation, too. We have a circular church, with the altar in the center of the church. It feels very different in one's body to experience one another in that roundness, for it symbolizes our unity and connectedness.

After the sermon, I felt extraordinarily blessed. I asked all women to come forward—women who were mothers, grandmothers, and great-grandmothers; women who were teachers and mothered their students; women who were mothers long ago; women in need of mothering. *All* women were invited. I wanted no one left out, so we all encircled the altar. We passed a bowl of water, each of us holding it for a moment, then passing it with a blessing to the woman beside us. In one beautiful moment, one of the women took the bowl and walked from the altar area to the pews, where her 99-year-old mother was sitting. As she came back with the bowl, there were tears in her eyes. Something so lovely was linked together in her gesture to her mother—the interwoven generations of all women.

After the blessings, I gave the bowl of living water to a young woman serving as acolyte; I asked her to pour it around the labyrinth that is right outside our large church windows. We all waited and watched as she honored Mother Earth, too. There was such completeness in the experience of those moments, gathering together women in all our forms, setting right and uniting so much that has been separated and unseen for so long. I felt the immense blessing of standing in a sacred altar space, the same altar space that was denied me as a young girl, a space that was, in another Orthodox church, deemed fit only for a vacuum cleaner. I felt, too, the blessing of the sacraments of an expressive priesthood that was denied me so many years before. Divine Mother heard me, and she opened up the altar space I had longed for—out in the world and deep within my heart.

I saw enacted the truth that I have always known, that if we have the opportunity to bless one another, to see each other as wise souls all on our own unique journeys, each with our distinct callings, if we give encouragement and space for our blessed vocations, then there is a balance that strengthens us in ever widening circles as we go out into the world.

After giving the Mother's Day sermon, the most amazing and unanticipated transformation took place—I no longer felt the compelling call to be a priest *in the church*. Divine Mother showed me that my desire to be a priest was really a desire to be one with Her, and I realized that I had had the connection with Her all along. My focus on separation, on exclusion and restriction and banishments, was a way of grieving, for me and so many of my sisters around the world, but in the necessary delving of that pain, I was temporarily blocked from seeing the fullness of Her surrounding me. Communion with Her was all I really wanted, and I would never be denied that. Callings are not for the limited few. The concept is not a top-down or one-size-fits all model. We all have our unique paths, our unique calls into the world—the diversity of our calls and our manifesting them is what makes this world a wondrous place.

All my life, Divine Mother has opened doors for me to fulfill my heart and soul—ways to meet and express who I really am. She shapes and blesses me, and I feel Her hand upon me. When something was denied me, she opened the door to learning and knowledge to satisfy my hunger. When I look back through all my years, I've had quite a long theological education, studying and learning and *living* all that I wanted to learn. My thirst for spiritual knowledge could not be contained in one individual program, and God knew that. I am a priest honoring many traditions, a loving voice in the world. The priest archetype that calls me is not the collared or robed priest, but the loving servant that so many in my family represented. I shared that with them, but I have my own unique vocation to express in the world.

I was shown that speaking truth through my writing, mentoring others, creating a healing space for people—these are the avenues for my call. As a storyteller, I need the freedom to speak with honesty and openness for my soul to be happy. My writing and teaching are ways I can speak truth, integrating all I have learned through my life. Each step along the way showed me that what seemed like a closed door often opened up the sky for me.

So, if I look at my dream in this way, then the dark man with the gun is a benevolent being, one who is opening my heart to my true self, helping me to burn off all that I do not need. It is the unconditional love and wisdom that both women and men can birth within themselves. All those who are initiated or become disciples of any spiritual path go through this process of transformation.

Jesus became *Christ*—a path of love over separation—and we are each entitled to be *Christed* in that Love. We unite all the parts of ourselves, and we release the fears that hold us back. We can get lost in the words or the names that represent something holy, believing that there is only one way. All traditions are holy—it is human limitation that creates suffering for others. But *agape*, the love that each of us can uniquely express in the world, is what Christ represents. Love always finds a way to make things right. The greatest commandment has always fed me:

Love . . . God with all your heart, and with all your soul, and with all your mind. . . . love your neighbor as yourself.[79]

Loving ourselves alongside God and neighbor—honoring our soul's call, claiming it, and loving others from within that claimed space. When I look at the many mistakes I have made in my life, I may initially feel regret, but then I pray for a shift in perspective. I pray that each time I am impatient or irritable that I be transformed from that point forward, that I remember to ask for forgiveness in the moment, or that I forgive others with the same swiftness. It is through our imperfections and our wounds that we can love others more fully.

Michelli Gomez taught me the wisdom of the Native American journey; according to her grandfather John Brumley

The earth journey is to be imperfect—to accept all that is.

This has been what I have perceived as my greatest shadow: my emotional sensitivity and judgment of self and others for what I have felt. I have judged my imperfections and because of that judgment, I have often remained frozen in those troubled moments. That should never be the focus. The focus is on the transformation, for

All things work together for good, for those who love God.[80]

This Bible verse has soothed me and guided me, not only to love, but to allow me to see how all things, no matter how painful in the moment, can work together for good. At times during my midlife recalibration, I have felt anxious about the mistakes I have made, anxious that I have not been worthy enough to receive God. But I know that my willingness for healing to take place makes it happen in wondrous and sometimes surprising ways. My intent for healing trumps suffering every time, if I but receive that fully in my heart.

So for me, the dark figure in my dream also represents Divine Mother, the Source of who I really am. I am born a woman, a woman made in the image of my God.[81] Without acknowledging our creative feminine aspects, we are not fully integrating an essential part of us. To do so means becoming one with our souls, when we are called to be tested, and going through our white-knuckled moments of doubt and fear. In those moments when there is no one else around, when the world as we know it is not known to us anymore, we have to claim what the Creator gives us: our wisdom and our gifts, allowing them to shine. We are not claiming ourselves *over* someone else. Our claiming bridges people; it does not divide them. If others are unaware or afraid of what we claim, we do not let their fear take residence within us. We claim ourselves and each person in the world over *all* of our collective voices of fear and doubt, while also offering up the suffering thoughts and pain we have carried for transformation—*the entire process* is woven together. No more fragments, no more compartmentalization.

One day, during the tornadic phase of the midlife call, I felt all of the spiritual truths and human experiences I had gathered swirl up through me. In my prayer time with Christ, I realized that *I* had been the one holding back. Yes, I had encountered many obstacles throughout my life, but when all of that was taken away and I stood alone before my Creator, I realized that I had to make the step forward to full communion. No more waiting. No more looking back and blaming anyone else. I wanted only Her, and I had to adjust my eyesight to see that She lived within me. I felt myself being pulled forward like a magnet. I saw Christ move to my side, making way for that connection. He smiled, showing me that Divine Mother was calling me to rest in Her arms and Her heart, that I was worthy of that communion. I knew that Christ was still with me, and I felt his blessing as I took a step forward toward Her. Christ wanted me to see that although he is my teacher and my savior, the one I call upon for anything I need, something in me still held back. He wanted me to see the clear image of his support of me to commune directly with Her. I had been dancing around Her feet for such a long time, but now was the time to become one with my true self. [82] That day, I felt my entire world shift its axis.

There were just a few lingering pieces of my journey that still needed to be brought to the light, brought to a full circle. The need to put words to some of the residual effects of the Armenian Genocide and the Feminine Wound still remained. The emotional heaviness of those stories still broke my heart at times. I felt like I had to walk through molasses to revisit those places, and yet I knew that if I put words to the heaviness, put words to everything I had witnessed, somehow I would be freed. I felt their mark upon me in the darkness, and they longed for expression. The strength of Her presence would give me the wisdom and grace for that outward expression.

Teaching a Child to Dance

Move with the music but
as if through water
with knees bent imperceptibly,
just barely, for grace.

Move your arms in joy
and let your fingers float,
following wrists as if through
waters that flow.

Let your hand trace a moonrise;
let your fingers harvest grapes
while we glide forward
walking like queens.

Bend slightly, move sprightly
with a springing step
in rhythms of the heart beat
with Anahid* and Naneh*
guiding your feet.

Move your hands
through the waters of Arax,†
palms down, then palms up.
Move with small glides,
magnificent child,
gift of waters and light.

And if you wave a kerchief
Wave it leaning back smiling
As if greeting hello and good-bye.

Look over your left shoulder
I am beside you.

And over my left shoulder
my grandmother and hers.
They walk like shy Christian
brides but behind them marching their pagan mothers
parading with shields.

Look toward your right shoulder
and into your future where
a mother-in-law smiles beckoning you into a life to be.
The Armenian dance is a dance of women,

Friends in a circle that opens
and closes and never ends. [83]

Diana Der-Hovanessian

*Anahid and Naneh are the names of women
†Arax is the name of a river

Genocide and the Feminine Wound

As a teenager, I read everything I could about the Armenian Genocide—I saw Henry Morgenthau's notes as Ambassador to Turkey, I read all the orders by the Ottoman leaders to kill the Armenians, and I felt ill. America, the country of my birth, still did not acknowledge the Armenian Genocide as fact. Politics and land seemed to take precedence over historic truth. Whatever was not healed for Armenians was still alive, still longing to be reconciled and healed. But without the right tools, it could leave us all stuck in another place and time, lost in a whir of images from our unfulfilled ancestors. All I could do was hold all the stories in my heart, in my body.

Healthy initiations often take place during adolescence, where we leave behind a naïve identity to live out more mature aspects of ourselves. But when initiations are *forced* upon us, especially upon young girls, a beautiful part of our souls is taken away. Opportunities to mature in healthy ways may have stops and starts—with some inner places that come to a complete halt.

Initiations borne out of a willing heart settle differently than ones that are forced upon us.

I think of the women in my family line who experienced a forced initiation into a new life, then had to find a way to survive and move forward. How many of us have been sent down a path that we have not chosen? It can take a long time—over many generations—to get back on track. I always knew that I had to put all the stories I heard about my grandmother, the many stories that shaped our family, into a book, but the emotional heaviness of such a task always loomed over me. To do so, I felt I had to go back to the point when the break occurred for each of us, the moments when choices were forced upon the women in my family. The repercussions settled upon us all. I had to revisit those broken junctures and make peace with them.

In Halep, my grandparents had many health issues that took their toll. My grandmother was once hospitalized just as my mother was going to perform in a school play. Her absence that day was one of many occasions when my grandmother was not present for my mother's creativity. My mother yearned for her. Time and again, my mother told the story of her mother's absence, of how it broke her heart. My mother could not bear to say anything but goodness about her mother, and yet all those unspoken feelings were still there, still calling out to be healed. I saw these stories and their feelings peek out many, many times.

When the opportunity came for my uncle to go to Jerusalem to study for the priesthood, it was hope for a new life for everyone in the family. My grandmother missed him terribly; he went away at age sixteen when my mother was eight years old. Seven years later, my grandmother and mother had their first opportunity to visit Kerry in Jerusalem.

Goodbyes were never easy for Armenians: they always hearkened back to the forced goodbye of a life and land that they loved so much.

My grandparents looked to my uncle to find a way for them all, and he took on that responsibility, too—he found ways for his family to have a better life, later bringing them to America. But when he was in seminary, it left a hole back home. My mother must have felt invisible at times, watching her mother cry and cry as she looked at Kerry's picture. No doubt she grieved for all the children she lost, and my mother saw and carried that grief with her, too. Mom loved her brother dearly—he gave her attention and became a father figure to her, but I also sensed what happens when one child is singled out to offer a way of hope for an entire family. Grief takes a front seat to emotional connection for the remaining children. These emotionally orphaned children do not understand: they just want their mothers and fathers to notice and to love them.

Once, when my mother was a child, a kind woman in their community offered to take her to the movies. It was a rare treat, and she said her parents gave her permission to go. Unfortunately, their transportation broke down on the way back, and Mom was late arriving home. When she entered the door, her father would not look at her or speak to her, and he kept his silence for two long weeks. A seemingly natural thing such as arriving late could not be taken as a learning experience, as part of someone's life journey, as an act that could be quickly forgiven.

In these moments, the brokenness of genocide and rape pierced through daily life and were passed down. An unspoken belief formed in the family, a belief that you cannot trust the world, that bad things can happen in any moment and change your world forever. Post-traumatic stress took its toll. My grandfather may have believed, on some level, that something horrible happened to my mother, that she would not return home to him. It may have triggered all the times he should have protected his family, and how he may have blamed himself for going back that second time. It may have triggered his intense grief over the loss of his three daughters, and my mother represented them all. But a child cannot fully understand why her father turns away from her, holds a grudge, or why she is at times invisible amidst her mother's endless tears. My mother often said that she longed to come to the United States, that she willingly wanted to create a new life for herself, that her childhood was too sad. She chose to see her parents with love and compassion, often saying

They did the best they could. They loved me so much.

She and I knew those words to be true statements, even as they walked alongside the underlying sadness and pain that still gripped her. My mother expressed grief and anger that her parents could not, and she did not know that I, too, saw and carried what she could not. I believe each generation that brings awareness to the pain in the family's shadow can chip away at pieces of it until there is no longer any left. But, each generation can also get stuck in the endless loop of pain, too. I have experienced both during my life. It is a tricky balance to express grief and anger, but not get stuck. Without the healthy expression of emotions within our communities, if we do not feel safe to use our voices to tell our stories fully, if we do not see reflected in our world that any mistake can be made right somehow—then the vestiges of stuck places remain in our psyches.

I think of the many wars, genocides, and holocausts of our time: Native American, Jewish, Rom, Kurdish, Rwandan, and Cambodian. The list continues on. It takes awareness and movement to bring about healing, to feel feelings, and to choose strength and joy. The saddest times for me have been when I could not magically give that awareness to those I love most in my family and my culture. But it is not a one-time event; it is a lifetime commitment to transformation. Each of us must make that choice for awareness and healing, and it also takes the commitment of a world community of non-Armenians to witness to the truth of our darker histories, to be willing to speak and learn from that truth as well.

Clarissa Pinkola Estés writes about the internal push-pull process that lives inside us when we experience war or trauma of any kind.[84] There is a hopeless feeling that the painful memories will remain forever, that each time we try to emerge, we will be pulled back down into a hole.

Yet with each moment of sitting in nature, of looking at life around us, we can begin to see something new. We must make room for it. Our internal psyche is a landscape we must cultivate. Clarissa Pinkola Estés shows us how to cultivate that land. [85]

Sometimes it takes extended periods of time when we do not show any outward results, yet take small steps breathing life into ourselves. Nature reminds us of vast possibilities that also reside within us. Preparing our inner ground is crucial for a new process to emerge.

I have seen the emotional wounds in those who survive genocide. Combine that with a feminine wound that makes a woman forget her unique strength and soul's discernment, and you might as well have a black hole, the wounds are so compounded. It should make us pause before we allow violence to infect the lives of so many people in the world. Each act of rape and war leaves its mark upon the emotional life of a family and a culture for a very long time. We love each other so much that some are willing to bear the scars of our actions until the time when we can learn a new way, until the time for others to gain the awareness they need. We can each help open one another's eyes, so that the loving sacrifice of so many souls can be used to make positive change in the world. Each person's journey affects us, in that it can be an opportunity, an invitation, for more love to grow. Suffering does exist, and even if some of us have suffered for love, it must not be the only path. Choosing to focus on the love of our souls over suffering is the link. That is the invitation of a bare ground.

Anything that is repressed only grows bigger until it sees the light of day. Formidable shadows have been following Armenians and Turks around for a very long time. It has long been time for some of us to shine light on what keeps us all so mired in the past.

I think about the present day people of Turkey who have not learned the truth of the Armenian Genocide, and have not allowed for that part of their history to come through and be healed. Armenians must allow for a greater sight, to see each Turkish man and woman as a unique soul who has a contribution to share with the world. *Their ancestors* committed genocide, so it is important not to blame subsequent generations for that part in history.

But subsequent generations can create an openness to heal the past, to hear truth, to create a bridge for healing to take place. Turkish people can open their hearts and ears to Armenians who need to tell their stories, to listen beyond the words to a greater story of reconciliation that runs through both cultures. Those who hear the deeper story can then help others move the emotional pain of a shared history. By choosing to open their eyes, to dig deeper, and to acknowledge a dark part of their history, the people of Turkey can create an opening to heal not only Armenians, but to free themselves as well. Again, commitment to a deeper soul listening not only helps build marriages, but also build cultures and communities.

I have seen it over and over again, how because of a painful emotional situation, we may lash out and see others in only one way—*us versus them*. By doing that, blame and judgment continue to feed, making it harder and harder to see our common humanity. It does not mean denying the facts of what happened, while grieving the immense emotional pain that needs healing on both sides; it means choosing not to stay in one point of view about someone or a culture.

Marcy Calhoun writes:

Once you judge [others] in any way that creates an idea of limitation about them or to them, you are karmically hooked into them until that judgment within you is released. Until you are willing to accept the fact that they are fine just the way they are, and you CAN understand why they are reacting as they are, the hook is still connected from you to them.[86]

On some level we are still tied to those whom we cannot fully see or accept. This is a tricky business, for it also involves allowing feelings, emotions, and words to be released about a painful part of history, while also releasing judgment about someone who inflicted that pain, honoring that person's soul journey. This may seem difficult to do in a given moment or situation. It does not mean agreeing with behavior that continues to cripple or devastate, nor does it mean forcing ourselves out of obligation to be loving when we are not. It just means being willing, in one small step, to move toward reconciliation, even if it seems impossible. It often begins with tending to vulnerable and inflexible places within us first. Yet full healing also involves speaking truth in the context of community. Truth spoken against injustice that is heard and acknowledged by one's community is a vital step for healing to take place.

Words of truth are not meant to break down a person's spirit, but only to unleash truth against a behavior that cripples.

Cultures and individuals who tend to look at others in a legalistic way can shift to a more inclusive view of others, when a community of truth-telling, forgiveness, and resolution is in place. This combination is what breaks through entrenched communication. If we have a judgmental *us-versus-them* stance, our energies are tied up until we are able to focus those energies in a more productive direction. That shift in perspective takes time, awareness, and an openness to the divine spark within each of us. Time and again, I have chipped away at the tendency to judge and to blame others—it is a willingness to break any habit that has become stuck. I could not rush the process, but I have had to revisit my willingness to embrace a life-giving outcome *over and over again*. Throughout my life, I have been shown that prayers of releasing outcome take many forms and move on many levels of awareness. With each painful release, I have experienced a much-needed forgiveness and reconciliation.

Such healing requires facing our fears. In the context of the Armenian Genocide, it may mean facing the fear of being seen as one-time aggressors in the history of the world, as well as facing fears of losing land, identity, or status. For me and for many Armenians I know, it is not about reparations or reclaiming land, and my sense is that it's not about that for our ancestors on either side. It is about healing something deeper—reclaiming parts of our souls. Once I had a vision of Turkish ancestors visiting me, feeling regret for what they had done to the Armenian people. I saw Armenian and Turkish ancestors standing side by side, both wanting the same healing for us all. It was a vision that surprised me, but then I began to see that each time we open ourselves to a greater vision of how love can move the world, our communities and our tribes will only grow larger. Eyesight becomes clearer, and one-time enemies will become brothers and sisters.

I think about Armenians who get stuck in their brokenness and loss for so long that they cannot see the good around them—they cannot see the goodness in life, cannot see that there are kind and gentle hearts in Turkish people who are open to healing this shared history. Some see every Turkish person as a perpetrator of genocide. Some Armenians judge others to protect themselves, but if we only see with the eyes of judgment, we miss out on the gifts and the divine spark within those around us. It takes strength and awareness on both sides to bridge that gap, to release the hold of a painful past. In the end, both sides must reach out to each other, to move toward reconciling what has been lost. It means allowing for our truths to be spoken without the hurt and anger that blind us to our shared humanity.

It may take a lifetime to heal, but step by step, it begins with two willing hearts. At times during my life, I did not understand how to do that. I felt the bottomless yearning that spanned back to many generations of women in my family. In an effort to be a loving caretaker myself, I felt the pull to mother when I had not fully been mothered myself. I felt both needs inside me. Many times, these needs would clash, and I found myself setting my needs aside. I know that my mother also did this— tried to give to us all that she did not get from her own mother. She moved forward in the ways that she knew how. We both did. Many women do this—we put our own needs aside for the sake of others, in an effort to bring healing for our families. Many generations of women have given from that place. Yet, if a woman only gives and never fully heals herself, there is still a wound that longs for attention, there is still a divide hidden for each subsequent generation.

I know my grandmothers, and the women far back in our ancestral line, felt the feminine wound of women in a patriarchal world. The inability of some of us Armenians to speak about the genocide, not only publicly, but also within own families, creates mute pockets in how we communicate within our relationships. How many times I believed others could magically understand my internal process, when I had only thought it in my head. Many oppressed cultures find ways to communicate with one another in coded messages. Africans who were kidnapped and enslaved in this country communicated through spirituals, songs of hope and freedom to one another. I believe Armenians have also passed down encoded messages to one another, through our prophetic dreams, our songs, and our stories. Because speaking truth has not always been heard or fully healed, stories were passed down to some as painful emotions or reactions, without a full voice. As a storyteller, I have had to listen for the stories behind the stories. I believe that my "heart attack" represented the last vestiges of pain and fear that my grandparents endured from the genocide—unresolved suffering that wounded all our hearts.

In America, having experienced an invisibility, some women create a coded language with which to communicate, until we find safe places to let our voices emerge. This is an imbalance that has been in our collective experiences for quite some time, and yet it has been moving toward more awareness and expression. Each time it gets balanced, each time we take a step to heal the wounds within by fully receiving what is necessary to feed our souls, balance begins to be restored in our society. Each environment that supports healthy and emerging voices expands the healing. Despite all the impediments, though, what I began to see is this:

The profound miracle is that despite our wounds, women have still been able to mother and replenish in such barren places, still have been able to suture what is so very torn. Even with gaping holes still needing to be healed, those who actively intend and trust in a loving outcome carry a vision of loving compassion in a tapestry of interwoven hearts.

My entire life, I intuitively knew that there was a way for *all* of us to be healed. Initially, I believed I was just supposed to do my part, to love others by filling an existing role left open for me in my community. I longed to create healing within the community, within the system, and any attempts at using my voice were not fully heard or encouraged. My vision could not thrive in that initial environment; it needed room to take root. Love is not enough to make change, if it involves seeing ourselves in a limited way. Limitation and lack are stuck places that can get passed down until we make the decision to see things in a new way, to move in a life-giving direction. The archetypes of caretaker and priest became vehicles for me to love and to serve. Yet if *any* role limits a person's soul expression, or prevents a deeper growth from taking place, then it is important to crack open the role, allowing for divine guidance to bring us more fully into the world. Sometimes it means temporarily leaving a relationship or community in order to gain the skills or greater heart to anchor healing for others.

When we have traversed a path of emotional pain for a very long time, we may carry the belief that any act of healing *never seems to be enough*. Armenians have carried such a burden about the Armenian Genocide. Subsequent generations have seen their parents and grandparents slowly piecing together shattered emotional lives, still learning how to find their empowerment. Some family members scramble to fix something that is far beyond their human capacity to fix, in an effort to save the family. Many survivors of the genocide relied on the help of their children to move them forward. Immigrant families often do the same—relying on their children to take on the role of communicators or providers for the family's survival. Yet one child cannot shoulder all that responsibility, cannot act as savior, for it not only affects that child's emotional growth, but also creates a pattern of having others look to that one person for something that can be cultivated in each member of the family. No one person can make the journey for others.

The emotional needs of some of us are so great that we can find ourselves getting lost in tremendous pain. As a child, I experienced this and did not know a way out. A gaping hole was present in my community. I noticed that no one seemed to intervene when part of me was dying, or when I gave too much of myself. By not intervening, I came to believe it was either expected of me to give too much of myself, or that I must find my own way, without guidance from others. I saw many Armenians living the same way, trying to make their way and not being fully seen by others. Many times I have seen women sacrifice themselves in order to give, while members of society also expected it. In many religious traditions, there are times when we are asked to give of ourselves at any cost. It is an unspoken expectation that lives and breathes within many layers of our society.

For years, I felt the emotions, holding stories of my ancestors in my body. I would use my words to try to explain what spiritual truths I knew—to try and bridge the gap for us all. Invariably, it left me tired and lost because I used too much of my own energy. I had to let go and allow for healthy growth and awareness for myself and others. But, if a woman has never seen that modeled for her by other women, if she does not know the sound of her own discerning voice, then by default, she may choose another's expectations over her own centered knowing.

As a child, I believed that the only way to love those closest to me was to sacrifice myself, to become the bridge for them.

In her novel *Rise the Euphrates*, Carol Edgarian shows the many forces that attacked an Armenian woman's sense of self. She tells the story of a mother (Mayrig) and her daughter Garod on foot during the Armenian Genocide. Led by Turkish soldiers, the Armenians have walked through the desert and have been marched to the edge of the Euphrates River. They are trapped. Mayrig sees no way out, yet her last instinct is to sing her beloved hymns. The Armenians around her fear the music will bring unnecessary attention from the soldiers, so a woman puts a kerchief over Mayrig's mouth, trying to stifle her voice, her creativity, her spirit. Carol Edgarian writes:

. . . Mayrig ripped the kerchief from her mouth, cried, 'Amot Kezi!' Shame on you! . . .' Do you think there is one among us who will not die? At least I swear I will kill myself and my daughter, too, before I'll allow us to be victims of the Turks!' Mayrig retied the filthy scarf over her mouth, and taking Garod by the hand she walked on.[87]

Those words have been etched in our collective souls as Armenians. *Shame on you* for speaking your truth, *shame on you* for wanting to live your life in the way you choose, *shame on you* for bringing attention to yourself, *shame on you* for shining your light in the world. Those beliefs have been passed down, along with the desire to defy them, to be the strong women we truly are. It is a push-pull of self-expression that gets tangled up—attempts and retreats until we women may get to the place of believing that we can only push the envelope so far before we have to put the kerchiefs back over our mouths. Anger has to be subdued somehow, or it will lead to the worst case scenario: genocide. Yet, the warrior still fights to find a way to hold onto something deep within. The horrible stories of how a mother is forced either to kill her own child or to see her child victimized by someone else becomes a place for that warrior to express herself. Against her will, a mother who is so broken may unconsciously commit crimes to retain whatever piece of dignity and soul she has left. This is the crux of the experience for some Armenians, wrenching dilemmas that live deep in our shadows.

In Edgarian's novel, Mayrig decides to jump into the Euphrates River, holding fast to her daughter's hand, so they can leap together. Garod resists, choosing life, even if it is not clear for how long. Just as her mother jumps in the river, Garod lets go of her hand:

The instant she let go of her mother's hand, Garod imagined she saw Mayrig fly, the orange kerchief rising above the water, like the plumb of a bird. Then, down Mayrig fell, into the muddy water . . . Garod searched the river for some sign of her mother and when she saw none, she looked overhead at the blanched sky . . . A child breaks irregularly, like a cup. Garod neither bellowed nor wept; the part of her that broke went numb . . . Close by, four women were staring at her. She saw what she thought was judgment in their mad eyes; she had betrayed her mother's last command, and for this they would condemn her. It occurred to her that even among the damned she was outcast: she was the girl who stood by and watched her mother drown.[88]

These are the choices that have lived in the Armenian psyche. When pushed to the limit, we may decide to shame what is natural within us: the beauty of our voices, the naturally flowing creativity that lives within us, and—perhaps the worst belief of all—that choosing life means betraying those you love. Because women have been so wounded, we may also judge and ostracize those who dare to want something more. These are the myths to break: that we will betray those we love when we choose to follow another road for our souls or to tell our own stories. We cannot help but speak, cannot help but add our own perspectives. We must remember that we *all* have an important story to tell, that there is a space for each of us, that it can be an inclusive circle. We can rebound when we search and find healthy sisters to show us the way. Armenians come from a long line of storytellers. Each time we create space to tell our stories from a deeper place within, we loosen the grip of judgment of self and others.

In her memoir *The Knock at the Door,* Margaret Ajemian Ahnert describes the mother-daughter storyteller process:

She was the narrator. I was her scribe . . . This is the story of us, told together.[89]

Over time, my mother and I began to write one story together. I held her unspoken stories, and some became my own. I had to sift through the ones that did not feed my soul, while also honoring the painful road she has taken. To add my own voice to our one story, it meant speaking to truths that were hidden for us all. I prayed for the wisdom and compassion to bring each of our stories to light.

I could not have learned self-compassion without taking time to heal each wound at my own pace, trusting my journey. I weaved my mother's and my grandmother's experiences in with my own, and began to see how each of us faced that hopelessness. I could trust a Mother God to be the guiding force for us all, and that prayer of letting go of outcome I learned as a child took its ultimate form.

In Edgarian's novel, the girl grows up to become a grandmother, naming the new baby girl before her, linking her to Mayrig and her hymns. The concentric circle of stories ripples out. She tells the baby all the stories, beginning in the style of Armenian storytellers:

Gar oo chugar, she began. There was and there was not.[90]

Sometimes before coming full circle with any story, you must understand the barren places, the places when *there was not*. Emotions behind a story need expression, need a safe place, so they can be channeled in a new way. Anger is one of those emotions. It is there for a reason, it has a truth, and when expressed and heard, it can take us to the next place on our journey. How many times I feared that if I expressed my anger, it would become a final resting place for my journey. I had to face that fear, too.

Your anger is your empowerment.

Carol Sydney

There are times when each of us must speak truth in the face of incredible odds and not back down, though fearful inner and outer voices constantly vie for our attention. Truth shared in this way may be judged by others as a threat, yet it is vital not to focus on fearful reactions, from within or without. Fear creates division, while love spoken as truth mirrors our true nature back to us. Allow anger against injustice to transform into a new form: a life-giving contribution for others.

Tina Karagulian

Outrage

For a period of time in my life, I could not see that I had any options. I felt victimized, not knowing how to change that perspective within me. I was angry at society for not modeling a better world for me, angry that women had not intuitively remembered how to do this for one another, angry that those I loved fell victim to patterns that kept them from peace, angry that when a person in a family system chooses healing, it can be seen as abandoning to those who feel broken and wounded.

I saw people choose addictions like food, substances, blame, resentment, or being right in order to numb the emotional suffering tied to this belief: that a painful story is etched in stone and cannot be altered. I have also seen people so lost in emotional pain that they cannot see the needs of others in their care. Those not conscious of the lost parts of themselves may unwittingly react to those around them. While I saw that in others, I also saw the same stuck places within me. Many times I tried to shift my anger and hopelessness.

D. Phelps describes this desire to move the rage as seen through a woman cleaning out her refrigerator:

I could feel the tension giving way to compulsion, as if by picking up and putting away, by emptying and throwing out, by wiping away the stains that could be seen, I could eliminate the ones that couldn't. . . . But the spill of this kind of rage compelled me to try again.[91]

I believe women have tried to find a way to move their rage for a long time. Without direct and gentle guidance from members of our communities, that rage can live inside, festering, hurting us and those closest to us. But, by seeking out those who understand the struggles, those who can assist in bringing about a healthy release, the rage can begin to leave our bodies. Wise women and men in our communities can show us how to see ourselves with more clarity, modeling ways to forgive ourselves and others. I had to experience full acceptance of myself and all my emotions, even my anger. One way of accepting my anger has been through listening to soul stories of women who have struggled with their rage and then found a way to resolve it. Reading about mothers of darkness in other religions has helped me to understand this important shift in action. It is through archetypal stories of the strength of the feminine—the creative and active parts that guide each of us—that we can find our way to the other side.

The Tibetan Goddess Palden Lhamo was a woman of unsurpassed beauty. A king married her and brought her to live with him in his kingdom. They had two sons. Each year, her husband ordered that a certain number of young people in the kingdom would be sacrificed to the gods, a ritual followed by all in the kingdom. Each year, Palden Lhamo pleaded and pleaded with the king to stop the killing, but her words fell on deaf ears. Finally, she offered the ultimate sacrifice. She said that she would kill her own sons, if the king would not relent. He did not, so she followed through, killing her own children. In the aftermath of the horror of her actions, she was devastated, wandering the earth, her hair matted and face blackened. No one could see the beautiful woman she once was. She sat on an ash heap, lost and brokenhearted. The Buddha of Compassion came to her and gave her the charge to be Protectress of the Family. She could not believe that she would be given such a gift—she felt so unworthy. But she had passed through the darkness and she was offered compassion. Ever since, she has been honored in Tibet as the revered Protectress of families and of a long line of Dalai Lamas.

Palden Lhamo is much like the Hindu Kali, often depicted only as destroyer. We see images of both of them with skulls, dark faces, and a fiery look in their eyes. But that is not the entire story. There is more to it than just the darkness and destruction, and it takes seeing with the eyes of the heart. Barbara G. Walker writes that sometimes destruction is necessary for women, but from that destruction can flow every kind of love and life-giving compassion. [92] It is important to see the fullness of our paths and not just one aspect.

I believe that Palden Lhamo, Kali, and the Black Madonna are linked together, collective archetypes that represent a maternal aspect that lives within each of us, women and men alike. It is the creative impulse within. This mother archetype is wisdom that brings us back to the dark earth, to our true source, to burn away creations and illusions we have birthed along the way—creations that *prevent* our souls from shining through. Divine Mother burns away that remaining pain and suffering that we not only created from identities we have chosen, but also identities and roles that have been passed on to us by the collective hand of our communities and histories. We carry those creations, illusions, and sufferings from our lives, and those not healed by our ancestors. *All* gets burned and becomes ash. We are loved and tended, picked up from the ash heap, and then we can begin to see clearly who we truly are. We can begin again. We create anew from a divine knowing, when once we killed our creative instincts. It is the purging and resurrection for anyone who follows a spiritual path.

I cannot deny that when people take something of our spirit by force— through genocide, abuse, or even expectation of service—we can forget who we are for a while. There were times when I was triggered to look at a new layer of healing, and each time it was an opportunity to discern what I needed for healing in the moment. Was it to speak my truth against injustice? Was it to heal my emotional wounds privately? Was it to remove myself from an unhealthy situation or person? If I felt particularly raw during those triggered moments, I had to tend to the rawness first. Eventually rawness moved to anger, which moved to expression of truth. I had to get to a point when the rawness would not prevent my truth. It took years to learn how to be tender and compassionate with my raw places, without remaining in blame toward myself and others.

Sometimes people around us can be catalysts for healing, even if they are unconsciously doing so. In such instances, we take stock with whatever is in front of us, and surrender to a deeper healing, wisdom, or awareness. It means believing that *everything* can be healed, even the raw moments. We may temporarily believe in the dark wound's power over light until slowly something shifts within us, and we see with greater eyes. One by one, we begin to see the traps that have held us back.

I once had a dream that my friend, a counselor like me, was driving a car with me in the passenger seat, when suddenly we went spinning in circles. I interpreted that to mean that when I *only* allow myself to analyze a situation, looking at it over and over again, it will drive my actions. I can be taken for a ride—and find myself running around in circles. I can get lost in the belief that nothing changes, feeling the hopelessness of the wounds of a memory. Having awareness, knowing the truth—these are important on the journey, but they can also become traps, unless after we speak our truth, we fully move into receiving what our souls need to thrive: to create by savoring the beauty of life, by receiving miracles, and by creating moments of gratitude.

It took me a long time to realize that blaming others can be a trap. Speaking truth as a way to witness suffering is so crucial, and it has been a big part of my journey, but the time came when I noticed that a kernel of the truth would not leave me; it continued to have a hold on me. I saw the patterns, yes, but I still felt pulled to be part of the very pattern that I was trying to clear. When I experienced self-doubt and saw myself as a victim, even in a passing moment, I could not fully claim my gifts. When I blamed others, there was a part of me, deep inside, that believed that they had control over my life. There were so many levels and nuances in this circular process that it took writing, sharing, and prayer to see it all clearly. I am in no way negating any part of my journey, for my desire for truth telling came from a desire to end suffering for others. But, I found that I still held the suffering and negativity in pockets within me. Being a holder of stories is not enough—stories need places to go, to breathe, to be in the world, *to show resolution.* That is the charge of storytellers.

I began to see that I can choose which stories to hold in my body—the stories of lack, abandonment, and victimhood, and the stories of strength, faith, and resilience. My grandmother's and mother's stories needed telling, the wide range of stories that filled their world, but I had to sift through them and add my own perspective—creating new life-giving stories, ones with possibilities.

Sue Monk Kidd describes how we can get stuck in the circle of blaming others as the object of our anger, yet encourages us to find creative ways to move that energy in order to empower other women.[93]

We may get caught in a web of not wanting to betray a person or institution, yet also feel betrayed by those unable to give what we needed. We may feel we are betraying them when we desire to move toward wholeness. It is only when we can move *beyond* betrayal, reaction, and blame that something else can occur. In other words, we shift our focus toward what we *want*, rather than toward what we don't want. Many of us say we want to move *toward* something, but something still pulls us back. For a time, it may mean wrestling with that until all the energy of that struggle changes form. Then a moment comes when we must make an active choice to bring all we are forward—all of our emotions and our experiences—into an integrated form.

Sue Monk Kidd makes it clear that the movement out of anger is not blind acceptance of an unjust situation, but transforming anger into healing and resolution for self and others.[94]

It can take some time to experience the rage within, to understand the truth behind it, before we discover how to move it. There was always a watchful part of me, knowing the loving and peaceful place I hoped to be, but another part did not want the pain to continue in the world, either. I wanted the truth of that pain to be seen, heard, noticed, and released. I knew there had to be a synthesis of experience for reconciliation to happen. Human injustice needs acknowledgement, so that it will not be repeated, but it can also lead to a stuck place of anger and loss. We have all seen this happen, to ourselves and to others. That is the point Palden Lhamo reached on her ash heap. She desired positive change, but she was not heard. She felt the anger of injustice, and she reacted out of that anger. Then she felt incredible remorse for committing the very act against which she had fought. When she could see that she had kernels of the same anger within her, too, when she could let go of beliefs and identities she no longer needed, when she was willing to forgive herself and others, then she could experience a true rebirth. She surrendered to something larger to be transformed. She was open to the compassion before her. In that intersection something else can grow—something green and tender can grow from the ash.

Sue Monk Kidd helps us to redefine the outrage of feminine injury so that it becomes green and new, so that we may find ways of relating to each other that previously were unattainable.[95]

Creativity is one way to transform and liberate anger, and we all have unique ways to create from our soul's center. Each time one woman claims her center, she is a model for others to do the same. I had lived my life trying to find venues, openings, and creative ways to move forward, while also allowing others to have their journeys. I have spoken out since I was a child, trying to make a difference. Yet, even though I tried building bridges to those I loved, I still had my blind spots. I had moments when I longed for a better world *right now*, in only ways *I* was envisioning it. I did not fully trust other people's timing, or the various ways that Divine Mother can create openings for others. Parts of me still wanted to control the process; I surrendered these lingering beliefs and blind spots within me before God.

For a long time, I struggled to understand the meaning of pride and humility. As a child I had a lot of wisdom, but struggled with how and when to express it. I was taught that my sense of self was too inflated, that I had too much pride, and that I needed more humility. There were times when this was indeed the truth. All my life, I struggled with finding the right balance. I watched how many people were so hurt that they could not hear a perspective other than their own. From their hurt place, they believed my vision was too inflated. It takes healing the hurt before an increased openness can occur. I had to heal my own hurt in order to open more, too. It took understanding the difference between pride, humility, and meekness. Robert Walden taught me this:

Humble differs from that of the word meek . . . Humility is self-honesty. It does not mean that you do not recognize or use your gifts.[96]

We, as humans, have weaknesses that we bring to the table, and being honest about them is very important. Yet we are also called to bring forth our gifts into the world. Not only do we need to embrace those gifts and tend to them, but we also need to express them outwardly. Holding back our gifts out of fear creates immense suffering for our hearts, as well as missed opportunities for others. That is when self-protection prevents Love from coming through us.

So many times I felt anger at the loss of my voice, at times perpetuating the belief that I needed to be meeker in the way that I used that voice. There are times I have spoken out of reaction and not out of love for another, too. Yet I also honor that regardless of the delivery, many times I *have* spoken truth to create an opening for someone else. It is an opening for a possibility to take place, whether or not it is seen or accepted by others in the moment. My role is to do my part, to help open that space. And if the opening is not welcomed, then I will not judge myself or others. There were times others have spoken truth I have not heeded. I see myself in every role, and I know we are all forgiven, no matter which role we have played.

I will continue to ask for love to be a companion to my words of truth. I remember Milo Beaver's words. I will honor that moment for what it is, knowing that God will take it from there.

When I was unable to censor my words during part of my midlife awakening, I realized that it was years of holding back, all those stops and starts as a young girl, trying to discern her world. Bob Walden reminded me to let it flow, even though I had a strong fear that I would hurt others. My sensitivity to others' reactions and my belief that I was hurting them had become a deeply embedded pattern of holding back my gifts. Yes, self-reflection is always important, but if that is all we do, we are missing out on living our lives. Each time I tell stories, I let go of any emotion, any fear, and any shame that may be connected with those stories. The stories of my life then become past events, a time when such-and-such happened to me, but then the stories no longer define my ultimate identity. The act of articulating words *is* necessary so that I may be free. As I spill out stories and wisdom, my words can become food for others.

The dynamics of victim and perpetrator fit the model of only one right and one wrong answer. Love can make more pathways, more healing possibilities than that. Painful experiences are never denied. They are felt, expressed, and are the seed for love in the world. Maintaining a judgmental view toward anyone maintains the dynamic of right versus wrong, and can contribute to a fixed, immovable perspective. I began to see the link between my not claiming my gifts and my judgment toward those who cause pain. Some of my actions were really *re*actions to fixed places in the history of my people. I wanted healing and resolution for those I loved, yet I had to learn loving detachment—that we are not responsible for how others view their own stories. Each person's soul will guide the way. I learned that I can live my own story, feel my own emotions, find my own healthy resolutions, and claim my strength. As I have done that, something takes over and, step by step, I begin to be more of a loving and compassionate witness to other people's stories— including those I did not think I could forgive.

If we continue to strip it down, we are given opportunities, over and over again, to choose love over every other focus.

I had been praying to Divine Mother, *I want something different to fill me now. Please, show me the way.* I prayed that I may be able to forgive all those who unknowingly caused those moments of suffering for me, in my past, my present, and my future. Within moments, I felt a warmth cover me, and I felt *Her* presence fill my heart. I thanked *Her* for taking the pain away so swiftly. *She* replied,

You have done your part. You have felt the emotional pain of all those moments. You have suffered much to get to this place, and your courage and awareness brought you here.

I felt *Her* blessings pour over me, and a much-needed completion finally took place. I know there are many more moments of healing and completion yet to come, but I felt that I had finally reached the other side.

My sensitivity, my perceived weakness, is what brought me to this place. My sensitivity is what broke my heart, yet that same broken heart was the opening that I needed ultimately to free me, to allow full forgiveness. What is left after this amazing alchemy takes place? A deeper form of love shines through, which is the essence of who I really am. My heart opened to more love and compassion than I could ever have imagined. Through the alchemy of love, the truth of our souls shines through like gold.

I had a few final steps to make on my journey. The time was finally right for me to speak *my* truth—not to cast out someone as separate from me—but to share my hurt, awareness, and truth once and for all, so that healing and reconciliation might take place. That yearning led me to a few important conversations.

Mama, we are going to have our own Communion Sunday worship service. Here. Now . . . I am your minister of communion today. You taught us about the priesthood of all believers—that each one of us is a minister of God. I am acting on that today . . . When Mama returned to church, the pastor politely questioned my authority to give communion. Mama smiled sweetly and replied, *Gestures of love are always appropriate, don't you think? Anywhere and everywhere we gather in his name, we can be ministers of the Master.*[97]

Olga Samples Davis

I learned this, at least, by my experiment: that if one advances confidently in the direction of his dreams, and endeavors to live the life which he has imagined, he will meet with a success unexpected in common hours. He will put some things behind, will pass an invisible boundary; new, universal, and more liberal laws will begin to establish themselves around and within him; or the old laws be expanded, and interpreted in his favor in a more liberal sense, and he will live with the license of a higher order of beings. In proportion as he simplifies his life, the laws of the universe will appear less complex, and solitude will not be solitude, nor poverty poverty, nor weakness weakness. If you have built castles in the air, your work need not be lost; that is where they should be. Now put the foundations under them.[98]

Henry David Thoreau

Truth and Forgiveness

One morning during my midlife transformation, I felt the desire to call Der Arnak, the priest who had denied me communion years ago. He was a family friend, a man I consider to be an uncle to me, a man who fought for women to become priests in the Armenian Church. His strong advocacy for the ordination of women almost cost him his position as priest many times. This man taught me how to break rules in order to bring truth and healing into the world. He taught me that it is better to act on behalf of your conscience and inform others later, rather than to ask someone's permission first. I needed to speak my truths to him, truths that I could not speak clearly years ago because I was so hurt.

I told him that his not giving me communion when I asked for it was *wrong*, that his role as priest required that he always give communion when asked. I told him how much I loved Christ my entire life, how much I spoke to Christ and to God even as a young child. I took seriously the act of receiving communion.

He challenged me, saying that he believed I was leaving one man for another. I said that though at that time my words no doubt sounded crazy to him, and though it caused many people a lot of suffering, I was led to be with someone who would understand my calling. I told him it was God who led me back on track.

He asked if we were married now, and I said we were. I said that I did not sin by choosing the right course for myself. Yet even if I *had* sinned, when I asked him for communion, it was his job to give it to me. Christ would never have denied his presence to anyone who asked for it, and he was wrong to deny Christ to me.

He challenged me, at times blaming me for things that were not mine to take on—decisions made by other people. Point by point, I reclaimed something back for myself. Something shifted in me as I reclaimed my truths. I became the voice I had hoped others would be for me when I felt so vulnerable. I became the strong woman I had been searching for in others all these years.

Then Der Arnak said something that was amazing to me. He said that my belief in Christ was far more than most of the priests he knew. Something broke through. He then asked me to forgive him, and I immediately forgave him.

The words that came through were balms of truth. I learned from a wise woman that it means *calling someone out*. How freeing to have words to describe my truth-telling process. What came through me as I spoke my truth was incredible love and compassion. It was bigger than me. There was room for truth as well as incredible love for all of us trying to make our way through this life journey. My heart felt that pulse through me as I spoke, and I know that even if every kernel of truth was not fully heard in that moment, the love that came through me was overwhelmingly felt. I readily gave forgiveness—it sprang from my heart without hesitation.

Truth, love, and compassion together are an incredible synthesis for forgiveness.

Could that conversation have taken place years ago? No. I was too sensitive to put the right words to what I knew were my truths, and I needed time to grieve generations of thwarted instincts and calls. I also knew that some things could not be understood until years later, when time would show that my choice to be with Pat was not a passing fancy or a wanton desire, but a union of two souls who were on a path toward embracing each other's calling.

Before hanging up the phone, I teased this priest, telling him that the next time I saw him, he was supposed to give me communion, even if it were grape juice and bread. Yet I knew he had already given me communion. When he asked for forgiveness, he gave me the communion that I had asked for years ago. I also gave him communion, too, by speaking words of truth to him, truth long held back. Resolution was fulfilled in that phone conversation, and a huge space was freed inside of me.

We have had many phone conversations since that day, and Der Arnak gave me permission to share that initial conversation within these pages. He gave me the opportunity to share a painful human moment, so that others could learn. I realized that what happened that day went beyond the individuals involved. It was about healing the limiting beliefs inside of me. Each time I wanted to move in a particular direction that nurtured my soul, something stopped me. Something hurt my heart. A lie formed inside me that said I can never fully enjoy moving in the direction of my soul. Through the dark places, I have retrieved those pieces, one by one. I have breathed into the life-giving choices I have made, sustaining them when others could not. I am the woman I have been searching for all these years. I am the support system that I have tried to find in others. Though I have needed to see that support system through my community, I also affirm that the strong woman lives inside me, in all her robustness. She was always there, guiding me. It took years to pull apart all the lies and all the distractions and all the pain to see her in her true light. She is the divine light that lives in each one of us, women and men alike.

Years of not being heard have created in me a shell of protection. My sensitivity over not being heard when speaking my truth created immense pain in my heart over and over again; in response, I chose to shut out the world. I know that, initially, I had no choice. I needed time to mend after years of suffering. Yet at some point, I found that I hid behind the sensitivity and self-protection. It went beyond the people involved and became a habit. I saw the same in many who had been hurt and unheard for so long. I had to ask myself, *Would I use my sensitivity as an excuse to shut down?* A hard shell develops that prevents other possibilities, miracles, or epiphanies to enter the heart. I began to see a difference: times when I suffered because of bad choices for my soul, compared to times I suffered because my inner spirit guided me to do so—for more love to enter. Both caused suffering, but discerning between the two was crucial for me to see. There are times I made boundaries against the first kind of suffering, but not the second. There are times we have to say no to what stifles our creativity and our souls. Yet there is also a point in time when we are called to move forward toward a deeper Love, *no matter how the suffering comes our way.* How many times I have hesitated, remembering that past pain. Yet when your inner strength and voice are intact, it is easier to bring forth Love. I felt my inner spirit reach back into every choice, every memory, and offer an open door, a way back.

What took me so long to let go of past hurts? I truly believe it is because I wanted to be heard through this human form, face to face, by others. I had approached all forms of release from every other angle, and yet this is the only one that remained. I learned to respect others, to wait for the right time to speak my truth. I had been given a gift of awareness, and I had to learn how to express it in a way that was the most loving. How many times I have been impatient, a bull in a china shop, in my effort to speak truth so it can be heard! How many times I could not hear someone else's inner voice and journey as a result.

Speaking truth and still holding onto hurt is not freedom. My dear friend Dru Dunn told me that there was a point in her life when she brought each and every moment of hurt before God, seeing in her mind the person who had committed each hurtful act. After revisiting each memory, she said, *And I forgive you for that.* She was finally ready to let go of each hurt.

I knew one thing that was true: I loved Der Arnak dearly, for he was my uncle and my brother. When I stepped back, I could see how he had played a role, so that I could learn to speak my truth. I could also see myself in all the roles before me: times when I was sensitive and times when I had been judgmental.

There are times when our sensitivity is so overwhelming that words are not present to express the truth behind our experiences. It takes gentleness and encouragement from within us to find the words that represent our wisdom, and then to express those words of truth to another. I have also seen when others have been so sensitive and did not yet have the awareness or understanding, and when my words of truth were not expressed in a loving and sensitive tone. We need practice to develop our voices in each situation—to voice the wisdom of our sensitivities and the wisdom of our minds. If two people are open to sharing that journey with one another, if we are willing to ask for more information and perspective from the other person, to be open to Love's full expression in both forms, then growth can happen. I needed practice loving others in the face of their judgments of me, remembering the times when I have been that insensitive and judgmental to others, too. The point is not just noticing the weakness, but the earnest attempt at becoming more and more open to love of self and others. Part of that integration for me was speaking truth with loving compassion—they merged together in a way that only divine grace can bestow. Love takes many forms and is the constant through each role we play, finally eroding every hurt until the emotions are spent and the need to hold onto our stories is no longer necessary. Loving truth is the constant that remains.

I'll give you a golden bracelet (the tools); it's up to you how you use it.

Dzoor nsdeenk yev sheedag khoseenk.
Sit crooked yet speak straight.

Which means:

It doesn't matter how we appear to others; instead, focus on speaking truthfully.

Zarman Meguerditchian

Holy Conversations

During my midlife, something led me to revisit crucial junctures in my life, and to see how they overlapped with choices my mother made during her life. Even though I made it my life's work to listen to and help heal other people's stories, my mother's included, I still had pockets of my own life story that needed resolution. It meant looking back at all my choices, all my mistakes, and all my longings without fear, without shame, without secrets. I wanted to be at a point in my life when I could speak to any hardship of my mother's and my life with both truth and tenderness.

My mother and I revisited the time before her marriage to my father, when my father asked her to marry him and she replied that she did not love him. He told her that he had love enough for the both of them, and after pondering his words, she agreed to marry him. Yet when she met his parents, she saw that something was wrong—my grandmother was unresponsive, and my grandfather said to her, *After you marry, you will take care of us.* My mother felt this impending doom, and after she shared her concerns with Kerry, he told her she did not have to marry anyone. I asked her why she married my father, then. She said she knew that his profession of love was indeed true, and it was a truth that she said never faltered. I asked if she married because she did not want to be a burden on her brother anymore, and she said that was true, too. But the larger truth, though, was that she made a vow to marry, and she could not go back on her word. What she said brought back to mind my grandmother's saying—*Dzoor nsdeenk yev sheedag khoseenk.* The importance of speaking truthfully over everything else was so much engrained in my mother, and also in me. I also have made vows that I felt I could not break, under any circumstance. I understood the background and choices that lived within my mother. They lived inside me, too. But there does come a time when we do not have to continue a course of action if it impedes our soul's growth. I chose a road that fostered healing and growth of my soul in ways that my mother did not choose. Yet during our conversation, I felt a healing compassion cover both of us. Something invisible was weaving together our differing perspectives and choices.

My mother shared with me how she cared for my paternal grandmother and grandfather just as she did her parents. But it took its toll on her to care for everyone. There comes a point in time when a supportive environment for self-care is needed, and if not taken, something shatters. Time to heal is important, but if it never comes, some never regain their strength. That happened for my paternal grandmother. I told my mother that Mama lost all hope long ago, but that I knew, on a deep level, that she appreciated everything my mother did for her. I told my mother about my dream with Mama, how she visited me and was alive, healthy, and her true self. How many times I saw Armenian women so sensitive and hurt by feeling abandoned, then judging those who were not there for them. I have done the same. It becomes a vicious cycle of hurt and judgment that further alienates women instead of fostering crucial bonding. If our individual voices fight to break through instead of shutting down, then they can be heard as the various levels of wisdom to *assist and strengthen* families and communities, not just to point out the weaknesses. Can we stop to ask one another for more information about our different soul journeys? Can we create opportunities for self-care to take place for one another?

My mother told me that she felt betrayed by what Papa did to me, and felt hurt that I abandoned her during our time apart. She could not understand my anger toward her then. I told her that when she spoke up against my Dad's anger, years ago, when she shifted the dynamics of our family, I looked to her to be my tiger mother. She admitted to feeling an uneasiness around Papa, but she did not listen to those promptings in herself. She said that had she known, she would have protected me. She never knew how to trust her inner voice, and I was no different. That is where our experiences overlapped. In the end, we were both women piecing together something that was lost for a very long time.

Sometimes I look at myself, my mother, and both my grandmothers, and I see us each of us as parts of one woman, trying to find full healing. We each have blind spots that have held us back. And yet, each time a woman breaks through to her own wisdom and shares that wisdom with others, she gives another generation an opening for more awareness and healing.

Some women and men in our family lost their lives and their way. Mama lost hope and gave up, as many of us do when we experience so much pain without resolution. Many of our sensitive Armenian poets, artists, and writers lost their minds after the genocide. Yet somehow I feel them all cheering us on to carry the torch they left behind. Each woman in my family line has had to face abuse and genocide in one form or another; each woman has had to find a time to rest and heal after long bouts of service, to resurface with an integrated self and strong voice. It is the path of this family line of women to achieve that. My grandmother Zarman gave us all golden bracelets, the tools by which to live. For me, it includes speaking straight, to the best of my ability, telling *all* the stories with as much love for us all, including myself. I pray that each young woman and man living today may find the tools inside to be true to their voices, while also making room for love. One cannot be sacrificed for the other.

My father used to tell my mother that she brought his family together. I know that my mother's voice is what initiated my father to break so many cycles of abuse. It was a call to some deeper healing for her family. My father listened. His commitment to live a better life kept his family together. His devotion to God and his love for us children broke through some of the darkness of his own childhood. It was an important step forward in healing the cycles of genocide's aftermath in his family history.

My charge also included speaking truth to the remaining holes that were left in that healing, to repair what was taken away in my family line, to honor the women who have had their bodies violated and their callings ignored. The final step for us all was learning how to express anger in healthy ways, to give words of truth in order to bring about healing, growth, and understanding with others—with a willingness to ask for forgiveness when we hurt one another. I am still learning how to navigate the slippery slopes. I know I will stumble many more times on this path toward reconciliation. But just like my dream, I have the tools needed to slide across the ice with ease. This book embodies *all* our shared wisdom, choices we have made at crucial junctures in our lives, and how the divine grace within each of us can show us how we can forgive ourselves and others in less time and with increased compassion. If we are willing to listen very closely at crucial junctures, to seek out the divine within for the right next step, to speak to wise women and men who will guide us, we will integrate all the lost and discarded aspects of ourselves. We will emerge strong, in full voice. I want my son to know that his voice matters, that he must never cease in finding ways to express his unique voice, and that owning his own mistakes and truly asking for forgiveness is a path to freedom. I know full well that Walden will make his own journey, his own time apart from his parents, testing his own discernment. He will discover truths that are only true for him, and he will teach his parents what we have not yet learned. I will continue to pray for divine guidance, asking that increased awareness, wisdom, and compassion be abundant for all of us. Our ancestors are present to cheer him on. Yet I am confident that the divine spark within him will guide him where we leave off.

The level of polarization in the world is such a huge divide now. It will kill us if we don't take a step. Have the courage to act from your heart. When you do that, more than you comes through.

Rosalyn Falcon Collier[99]

I had a great chuckle the other morning when as I awoke from a dream, I heard myself proclaiming the words: We are on the threshold of something new. *With all that is going on . . . those words were certainly not a new awareness. But the humor for me was in the invitation to* Wake up, get up and get going!

Jean Springer[100]

Reconciliation—the Circle Widens

Reconciliation means standing true in our voices, while also growing our hearts beyond our wildest dreams. I have searched out many who have been able to bridge these two seemingly disparate concepts. In Rwanda, perpetrators of genocide served time in prison, then came back to their communities in order to hear full accounts of how their actions broke the lives of others. Each family member has a chance to speak out before the perpetrator, in an effort to come together again as a community. Often, those who burned down homes would then rebuild them in an act of reconciliation. It has been an incredible model for us all to witness, allowing truth-telling, forgiveness, and acts of reconciliation to be linked together. I wonder about the many ways we can rebuild our inner homes, our souls, in the same manner—both sides willing to look at themselves, willing to be aware of the barriers to reconciliation. As was demonstrated in important conversations in my personal life, there is a time when we are ready for that deeper listening. When the time comes for that conversation, both sides must be willing to let go of something they held onto, so that healing can occur. Words of truth *combined with* loving and opening hearts—this is how lasting reconciliation can occur.

Several years ago, at a dinner with friends, I was asked to relate some facts about the Armenian Genocide. After I did so, my son Walden, a young boy at the time, boldly proclaimed,

My mom hates Turks!

I was stunned. Did I relay more than historic fact? I wondered if his words were pointing out something within me that I could not see. Were there negative emotions behind my words? Were there spaces within me that needed transformation? I decided that I needed to have more one-on-one conversations with Turkish people who were open to speaking from their hearts, open to bridging whatever was stuck in my consciousness. I told Narjis Pierre, a Muslim friend of mine, of my intention. She knew the history of the Armenian genocide, and she knew many Turkish people in her community. Narjis matched me with the right person, one who would be open to such a conversation. She arranged for me to meet a Turkish woman for dinner, and we met at a Middle Eastern restaurant. Her daughter and my son sat at their own table, sharing a meal and game together, while we focused on our own conversation.

I was nervous before I arrived, hoping that my heart could remain open to both her and me, that I would speak in a truthful yet gentle way. I prayed for that ability, and I know I received it. I watched this amazing woman open her heart to me. During her childhood, she said that she lived in Turkey in a remote village. She noticed that in one part of her village, there were houses that were boarded up, and that there were people digging in the back of each house. She innocently asked her mother,

Where are the people who lived in those houses?

Her mother told her that the people abandoned their homes. That is all she said, and it left a pregnant space in the room that was palpable only to her daughter. She knew there was much more to the story and she was open to hearing it. I was able to fill in some of the gaps for her, telling her that many Armenians hid their gold and jewelry in their backyards for the time when they could return and resume their lives, and that in some villages, Turkish people began living in Armenian homes that were vacant after the genocide.

As we talked, I noticed that something shifted within me. I saw a woman willing to open her heart to me, open to hearing my part of our shared history, open to revealing what her discerning voice within had always known. Hearing her inner voice speak liberated both of us. I was able to validate her discernment, and she was able to hear the truth of my story. There was no judgment between us, just a desire to make sense of a shared past history.

Something loving and beautiful began to grow—far greater than I had imagined. It took two open hearts and a loving conversation. To the outside world, we were just two women having dinner. To anyone who feels hopeless, it may only seem a small step that can in no way change history. And yet, we were there to witness love's transforming power. Each of us had an important role in that reconciliation: Narjis had the awareness to match two people *ready* for that conversation, for she was part of an outer community willing to create a space for healing, and each of us came with an open heart, awareness, and willingness to hear the other's truth. It seemed to me to be a blueprint for reconciliation. And it began with my son's words of truth, asking me to be aware of the shadow within me.

When I look back at my life, I can see that I have been on all steps of the journey; I have played all the parts. I have expected others to heal the wounds that only my Creator could, and I have had to learn to redirect that expectation. I have felt abandoned by those unable to give, and I know others have experienced my abandonment of them. Yet I have been forgiven and loved by many people, including my Creator. These are the constants of my life.

Many times during prayer when I have been lost and confused, I have heard Christ's words ask me,

What are you afraid of?

After I get it all off my chest, I often hear,

No one judges you here. Forgive yourself.

If I allow it, my heart is then filled with incredible peace. Many times I have heard Christ feed me a song lyric, often a line that would crack me up! I have laughed out loud, and often heard some snickering on his end. These surprising moments teach me that there is a lot more love and joy *and snickering* that goes on in heaven than we can imagine—a heaven that lives inside each one of us. I smile back and realize that whatever is weighing so heavily on me is not as important as laughter and love.

In my counseling work, I have rejoiced in the healing journeys of women, listening to them as they have healed their injured instincts, in the step-by-step process of reconnecting with their soul purposes. Every time I see a woman stand taller, I know that we all benefit. Each time I love and claim myself, I offer that to the world, too. I am so grateful for the outer circle of women who have loved me. I know there have been many who have been there for my mother, too. We are a vast circle of sisters, each reminding us of our true potential.

Those whose lives may have been cut short through violence from their communities, or through forgetting their own inner voices—they are still alive through us, inside our creativity and our life journeys. Their stories have come up from the ashes to fuel my words, to live on in a way that feeds others. I know that at the end of our life journeys, *all* of us will be led back to our shared Source—the magnetic pull for us all. I have been told that in the end, no one will be left out or forgotten. This knowledge, time and time again, has brought me immense comfort.

The moments I forget this truth, I have to stop and slow down. My full vision of others may be the only centered action that I can offer in a given situation—visualizing their divine strength and seeing it guide the way. We can choose to see *possibilities* instead of loss, and we can re-remember that we are more than any pain we experience. With each remembrance, a deepening compassion grows.

Mahatma Gandhi[101] knew despair, and I have cherished his words to help move my own:

When I despair, I remember that all through history the ways of truth and love have always won. There have been tyrants, and murderers, and for a time they can seem invincible, but in the end they always fall. Think of it—always.

When I despair, I have allowed myself to forget love. There are times I have allowed another's belief in despair to reside within me. At these times, I often feel heaviness in my heart or spine, or pain in my body. When I slow down and increase my awareness, I can see the moment I allowed despair's entry into my consciousness. Betty Eadie reminds us,

We are not to deny the presence of the illness or problem . . . we are to simply deny its power over our divine right to remove it.[102]

As I have learned to embrace my divine right to remove any impediment before me, I receive what I need for my soul and it ripples out as love for others. Over time, a divine love takes up more and more residence within me, and I respond less and less from my reactions and triggers. Love transforms them all. I learn when to intervene, when not to, without ever stopping the flow of love.

Love takes many forms of expression: service through prayer—any form of connection or communion to the divine in us, *then* an outward expression of that service in the world. Sometimes after a moment of prayer, speaking strong words of truth are necessary, while other times being a silent yet loving presence may be called for. Whatever life journey we have lived, whatever heartache we have endured, there is a way to bring what we have learned to others. We each have a unique way of expressing that love, and when we choose the right form for our souls, we feed others, *including* ourselves. Whatever has been stuck can become cooked into food for all.

When our souls are truly fed, this is the most important form of reconciliation.

The dream that shook me awake, that left me in a sweat, was my soul calling me to come full circle. In the dream, I was afraid to meet what was remaining in my shadow. I was afraid that breaking open my heart to its fullness would be the death of my soul. I initially ran from it. I was running from my vulnerability, my weaknesses, my anger, and my nakedness before God. I thought I could only look at a few parts of my life, while judging or ignoring the rest. Yet when I faced my vulnerability and my fears, when I offered loving compassion to my *entire* life, I was led to integration. The divine has been with me throughout each moment of my life. I have surrendered each painful moment and belief so that I can be freed, a forward movement that I have not always seen as in motion. And yet I have felt that motion when I walked alongside other people's stories, at times when I held their pain in my heart, and the times I blessed the stories as I released them.

At times I have been dismissive of my own grief and wisdom. I have made mistakes, and I have hurt others. I have felt collective suffering in my heart. I have spoken out against injustice in hopes that history would not be repeated. I have learned that when I make mistakes, I can forgive myself immediately. No more running, reacting, or blaming. All of these parts of me I bring to the table, and I accept all of me. With love, I will not see wounds or genocides as looming figures; with love, I can see the constant miracles in my life and in the lives of others. Then I can see what Gandhi sees.

Love *is* enough. How many times Christ and Divine Mother have repeated to me that I do not need to *do* anything in order to be loved. It took some convincing that

I am loved, I am enough, and my love is enough.

As I finished writing this chapter, I knew that this was the beginning of a phase in my life that would bring about joy, corny humor, and more love. It's as if a sweetness has now taken residence within me that can never be taken away. New experiences and creative endeavors carry a lightness now, for the burdens of the past had been met, blessed, and integrated. Moments of sadness do not linger. I pause to feel warm and expectant soil between my toes, stepping into the unwritten now.

All Matter of Communion

I see altars and communion everywhere now—
the amniotic sac
a suspended place
where communion travels
through nourishing liquids
of an umbilical cord.

I watch the moment when
a woman bends her nipple,
ever so gently,
into the mouth of her babe,
much like the goblet of wine
is tipped so that we can drink.

I see our crossing guard
wave and smile to passing motorists,
offering a good morning greeting
to each child she guides,
and as they cross the street,
with her protective hand held high—
they have been blessed
by the richness of her communion.

I watch a female cardinal
bend her orange beak
to her fiery red partner,
giving him not only seed
but a lot of love thrown in.

I notice when one offers a flower,
a piece of fruit,
or a smile to another—
I see the offering transform

the face of the other,
in quiet wonder.

I marvel at all the altars
and passing of communion
that take place
within each moment,
within each day.

And in case we forget
that God is infinite in Her giving,
She enjoys dropping another surprise our way,
like a love note you put in someone's lunch,
and all we need do,
is notice.

Tina Karagulian

Diligent Joy

Happiness is the consequence of personal effort. You fight for it, strive for it, insist upon it, and sometimes even travel around the world looking for it. You have to participate relentlessly in the manifestations of your own blessings. And once you have achieved a state of happiness, you must never become lax about maintaining it, you must make a mighty effort to keep swimming upward into that happiness forever, to stay afloat on top of it. If you don't you will eat away your innate contentment. It's easy enough to pray when you're in distress but continuing to pray even when your crisis has passed is like a sealing process, helping your soul hold tight to its good attainments.[103]

Elizabeth Gilbert

Divine Feminine

My longing for God as a Divine Mother has brought *Her* to me in so many ways that I begin to see *Her* everywhere. I see her in Erma Crumedy, the crossing guard in front of my son's elementary school. Her beautiful dark skin and shining smile show me that she is also a dark mother, another Black Madonna. She encourages each child she sees, making sure they know they are loved, that they can start their day on the right foot. She and I often share our life stories with one another, and she teaches me the power of speaking truth out of love, the power of forgiveness in her own life, and that God will always lead the way. One day, she looked me in the eye and boldly said,

Tina, it is your season.

How does she know it is my time? Has she been talking to my grandmother? I smile. Each time we claim our calling, each time we claim our divine voice, it is our season, our time to shine in the world. I believe that when we women and men claim our divine voices, we will have the keys to our collective healing, the key to improved relationships, the key to peace. Call it what you will—it may be the creative muse within us, the strong voice that fights injustice, the truth that clears the air when nothing else will. We each have a unique way of expressing that in the world.

It has taken years of entering and reentering the dark cave of my heart to find *Her*, yet it has taken me this long to claim *Her* fully within me. I remember Tiran Surpazan's words heralding the right time for something to move forward. I have had to trust my internal process, a timing that was unique for me.

My mother and I had been reconciled for a long time, talking regularly and visiting one another. Both of us have grown, able to heal and see one another in a way that is more heart-centered. But there was a final step that I wanted to take. I decided that during my next visit home, I would not stay at a nearby hotel, but at my childhood home. I wanted to sleep in the house that held so much terror for me as a child, and I wanted to transform any remaining beliefs embedded in the feminine wound. I prayed to a Mother that was greater than us all to heal each room, each moment, so that the home would be fresh and new for all who entered. It was a reclaiming of my childhood, and a way to show my love for my mother. During that week, I tended to myself and others. I felt the heaviness of memories long past, and though it was difficult at times, I saw how much divine grace could fill me and my life. I allowed for that transformation, and saw the strength of my soul shine back. I spent time with each member of my family, showing my love for them as they live out their individual journeys.

My mom cooked for her grandson, something that brought her much joy. I have watched my mother over the years, tweaking recipes into masterpieces. No one can make *yalanchi dolma* with such perfection— her grape leaves filled with rice and secret concoctions that are rolled up and served cold. It is through that creative impulse that she has created offerings not only for her family, but also for her church community. She is also a storyteller, like her mother, and I took on that role in a way that was true to my soul. My stories were my recipes, and I needed opportunities to prepare those recipes in my batch of wisdom. Each time we are willing to listen to one another with that kind of attention, the barriers to love fall away. Each time we speak our truth with love and strike the right balance, our recipes are perfected, and we all are fed.

My mother has given me her blessings to share my stories, even the difficult ones we both shared together. I could not write this book without her blessings, and without her continued attempts at understanding my journey.

I told my mother that I recently shared my grandparents' reconciliation story before an Armenian community. It was the second time I had publicly shared the story that had been etched in my heart all these years. As I retold the reconciliation story in front of the crowd, something welled up within me, giving a pregnant pause before I continued. It may have appeared to those around me that I was emotional about the genocide, or emotional about the pain that was inflicted upon my family, yet it was neither. I felt incredible love for my mother as I was telling a story that both she and my grandmother told. I was being initiated as a storyteller, too, in that moment. It shot through my heart in such a strong way; I felt the divine spark that connects the three of us women together. I told my mother that I felt this incredible love for her right then, and she and I both cried tears of joy.

During my visit to my childhood home, I watched my mother slow down to rest, something she rarely did most of her life. She has learned to create a space for herself, regularly reading the Armenian Bible that Kerry gave her long ago. She said that now, whenever she is anxious, that act brings her peace. What a gift to hear that she is able to have peace. I knew that our prayers for one another never stopped during our time apart, and I know that those prayers brought about the reconciliation we have today. No doubt my grandmother had a hand in bringing about that healing for us. I have carried the stories of the women in my family, giving them a resting place within these pages; Divine Mother's blessings have been upon us all.

During the visit home, Walden and I spent the day with my sister Lisa and her son. Lisa and I walked to the elementary school of our childhood, watching our boys play on the swing set. I looked at the now empty place where my favorite tree had stood. I remembered the days I used to climb the tree and rest in its branches. How it mothered me. I think of it fondly, seeing it as a sister tree to the one that my grandfather climbed so long ago in *his* childhood, claiming it and the land over all else. Somehow the trees connect us to one another.

The four of us decided to go to a local farm to experience the fruits of the season. I craved apple cider donuts, the fresh autumn air, and brightly colored leaves. We have wise, sensitive, and loving boys—another generation that will lead the way, full of promise and hope. We mothers attempt to fulfill what was missing for ourselves, making the road easier for our children, and yet God will watch over them as they find their own way, too.

Walden and I walked beside a lake filled with quacking ducks; suddenly, we looked up to see a blue heron fly over us. It reminded me of the one Pat and I saw in the greenbelt when we first got together. Yet as this one flew over our heads, Walden called out that he saw something shining in its beak. Sure enough, it had caught a fish with bright orange scales that glistened in the sun! It had found its gold. Herons always wait for the right moment to seize an opportunity, to take what is rightfully theirs. I feel that I have found this within me, too. But these gifts are not just for me. I cannot not help but affirm that

It is our *season.*

On my last birthday, I decided to go to the beach for a weekend of solitude and refreshment. I reveled in the salted air, while the waves crashed at the shoreline. To my surprise, I saw a beautiful yellow butterfly flutter its wings near my face. It looked a lot like the one that visited me after Kerry's passing, reminding me of his rebirth into new life. Yet this butterfly also amazed me. I thought to myself,

How could something so delicate flap its wings in such a surging wind?

I thought of every woman who has conquered the feminine wound and reached the other side. She embodies delicacy and strength in any situation. In the claiming of herself, she becomes a wise woman. Each time a man listens to the wisdom of women, and each time he listens to his own internal rhythms, a beautiful transformation takes place.

Clarissa Pinkola Estés teaches us the importance of following nature's rhythms as they mirror our own.[104] It moves us out of time into the time of our souls.

Native traditions also teach us to look at the patterns in nature—to animals that represent a strength we can develop in ourselves, or a gift we already possess. Ted Andrews writes that

The animal world has much to teach us. Some animals are experts at survival and adaptation . . . Some are great nurturers and protectors . . . Some embody strength and courage, while others can teach playfulness. The animal world shows us the potentials we can unfold . . . They show us the true majesty of life itself.[105]

The vulture and the whale have guided me to understand my roles in the world. The vulture is one who clears the earth of what is left behind, taking away germs and disease—often seen as the gruesome part of death—in order to make space for something new.[106] I have played this role in my life, walking into dark places for myself and alongside others, clearing a space for healing. Most people think vultures are ugly when they look at them up close, not understanding their purpose or respecting their role. But when you see vultures soar in the sky, you see their beauty shine. You see how they can glide on the air currents, their movements graceful, and the tips of their feathers like fingers longing to touch the sky. They have a perspective and a vision that is higher than most birds. They call out to one another, so that they can share what they see, so that they can share an abundant meal with their community.

The whale is a keeper of the records of the people, the one who holds the stories—the wisdom, the joys, and the horrors of the tribe.[107] I have held ancestral stories, yet I also know that when we peer into other family systems and cultures, there are always others who do the same: the truth-tellers and story-keepers, those who feel the impact of stories in the cells of their bodies. When communities recognize and honor the unique gifts of *all* the members of their groups—the truth-tellers, story-keepers, and wise women—healing is possible for all.

Whales express an abundant joy into the world. They are majestic beings who love to play in the waves, who love to jump fully out of water and fall back into the water's embrace. They playfully blow out water through their blowholes, and slap the water with their fins. Whales help me to remember that I do not have to hold all the stories of pain, that I can blow them out in creative ways. Whales remind me that joy is the essence of who I really am, and expressing it in the world is all that I need do.

D. Phelps describes what it is like on the other side:

I knew there would be a storm there, and that annoyed me, so did the cold, usually. But today, I had a new understanding, and my life would never be the same.

'Do what you will,' I said to the sky. 'I am finally warm. [108]

That warmth is what I heard in the divine call, beckoning me with the words:

You don't have to give up anything or any part of yourself when you speak. I will send you places that you never thought imaginable.

How true that has been for me. As I weave all the stories of love and truth within my heart, I feel my grandmother's presence filling in the gaps, not only for me, but for my mother, my sisters, my cousins, and future generations. She does not want unhealed moments of trauma to stay trapped within us. She longs for cohesiveness so that we can move forward, and from where she lives now, she has a better vantage point.

The following pages hold the prayer she has given me, a call for each of us as we find our way:

It Is Time

You are the fruit of all my loss—
You take my heart to the valley in Zeitun,
where ripe olives burst in your mouth.
You are my life,
which continues to live through you.
No desert can take away my longing
to find you,
to love you.
I *could not* rest until all was put right,
through you,
through my children's children.
Such is a mother's love—
Anger and hate cannot consume it.
Our souls are bolder,
brighter,
and more resilient than hate.
I—am—your—grandmother!
You are my blood,
my heart,
My Zeitun Warrior.
Pure strength and love—
this is our legacy.
My insistent voice is the voice of all mothers
who fight to hear and to be heard.
Your mother yearned for me through you.
I could not fully see or hear your mother.
I feared losing her, too.
Many of us did that.
That was not living.
It is time to unleash that fear.
You are so *very* loved.
No one is left out,
not you,
not your mother,

and not any Turkish woman or man.
God's love is big enough for everyone.
Guh hasgunas?
Do you understand?
Ayoh, guh hasgunam.
Yes, I understand.
I am the proudest woman,
watching my own flesh and blood
heal what I could not.

It Is Time.[109]

Epilogue

It was Valentine's Day weekend, and I was rushing about to collect fun dessert items for a small get-together with friends at our home. I purchased chocolate truffles, strawberries, and ginger cookies, along with necessary items for the week. Yet as I drove off, I realized that I forgot to purchase the mango sorbet, an item that Pat had requested. I knew that it was very important to make that wish come true. I eyed a small store on my drive home, walked in and went right to the mango sorbet. Mission accomplished. But as I walked toward the counter, I noticed a jacket hanging on the rack nearby. It was a butterscotch-colored, faux leather jacket—exactly like the one in my dream! The dark man who wore that very jacket broke open my heart to love in a deeper way, yet he also had a great sense of humor. So, here I am on Valentine's Day, the day that honors love and sharing of hearts. I faced the fears that told me to deny parts of my life experience. Instead, I picked up *all* the papers of my life, honoring each story for its importance, holding them close, where they could be met with love and humor. I knew that in my life, even times when I would resist that integration, I still moved forward. Nothing can ever stop that. I smiled, seeing the inner and the outer experiences come together. I knew that what lay before me were more and more reconciling moments of love and laughter, and through my creativity, through my interactions with others, I would share them with the world.

Appendix A

Renunciation Sermon
by Tina Karagulian
September 9, 2007

In the Gospel reading for today, Christ says, *. . . whoever of you does not renounce all that he has cannot be my disciple.* [110] Christ asks us to give up an idea of who we are, give up our identities, give up what we are comfortable with, in order to fully receive the Divine. What do you identify with, and does it keep you from serving God? When we let go of what we don't need and seek to receive our true calling, we may experience pain in the releasing, but we also receive so much more in return.

I want to tell you a story.

Once there was a woman who lived and worked in the valley between two mountains. She farmed the land with her family, she was strong, and she had one son and three daughters. She went to church every Sunday. One day, she was told to leave her home. Some of her neighbors were being killed. She took whatever possessions she could carry. She left her youngest daughter with a neighbor because she thought her child would be safer there. She and her remaining children, husband, and extended family were forced to walk through the desert. Armed guards would steal whatever gold they would find from those who walked. The sun was very hot during the day, and the nights were very cold. With no shelter, the elements were harsh on the body. Soon there was not enough food or water, and people would die along the way, with no one to give them proper prayers or burials. Young girls were often raped, so many parents would cut their daughters' hair in order to disguise them as boys. The woman who left her daughter with a neighbor heard that the neighbor was *also* forced to walk with them; she searched frantically and miraculously, was able to find her daughter. Her daughter looked angrily at her for leaving her behind; she was too young to understand. Unfortunately, because of the hot sun and lack of food, this daughter contracted a disease and soon died. The woman's two other daughters also died. Finally, this family survived the journey, ending up in a distant country as refugees. Different churches offered food to the refugees if they would become members of those churches. But this woman chose to keep what was left of her identity, which was her church, a church that went back to the time of the apostles, because her faith is what got her through her ordeal.

This is the story of my maternal grandmother, whom I never met, but whose story I have carried with me.

At one time, half of present-day Turkey was once Armenian land. In 1915, the small, secular and nationalist leadership in Turkey called the Young Turks set out to exterminate Armenians in the first genocide of that century. In my family, we were lucky that a kind, Turkish man saved my grandfather's life, alerting him in the middle of the night, for he was to be killed in the morning. Yet, even with such kindnesses, approximately 1 1/2 million Armenians were killed. To this day, the governments of Turkey and the United States do not officially recognize that the Armenian Genocide took place.

These stories were truths I learned as a child, that terrible things can happen to your family, to your identity, but that the truth of God and church were stronger. For me, the Armenian culture and church were so connected that I didn't know there was a difference until later in life. The Armenian Apostolic Church is an orthodox church founded by the apostles Thaddeus and Bartholomew. Armenia accepted Christianity as a nation in 301 A.D., and its church service includes the Nicene Creed. The Episcopal Church is seen as a sister church; the liturgy is so similar.

Growing up, I listened to the beautiful Armenian church music. I found something beautiful amidst the shame and sadness of my culture. The music took me beyond the labels and limiting beliefs that came from the genocide. The church service spoke of the light and love of Christ and God, and I actually felt that love. I dropped out of Sunday School to join the church choir at age 16. It just felt right.

In that same year, I attended a church retreat in New York and remembered being drawn to the bible verses and to the liturgy. I felt that I was home. I befriended another young woman who felt as drawn as I did. We had lectures during the day and prayer every evening. I was on fire. Then the day came when I asked a question and the speaker made a comment that women could not become Armenian priests. I remember the life being kicked out of me. I didn't know it consciously for many years, but on some level, I felt called to the priesthood. I realized that although I felt this incredible pull to serve God, those around me could not see it or allow it. Sadly, a young Armenian girl could only go so far within the Armenian Church.

I decided that I could not force what is not meant to be. And yet, I kept feeling a call to serve. My first internship in college was in a day treatment program for people suffering from mental illness. I didn't know what to expect. I found out that just sitting with others and being fully present with them made a big difference. On the last day of my internship, I said my goodbyes to everyone in the group, and one man spoke up. He often spoke in sentences you did not understand, often "delusional" as others put it. And yet, in that moment, he was very clear, commenting on my sincerity and thanking me for being there. I knew then that I made a connection, that I was serving God. I was listening to the stories of others, *people I did not know or grow up understanding*, but I was honoring their soul. I was where God wanted me to be, to understand the suffering of others and see their souls as equal to my own.

I continued my education to serve as a clinical social worker. I was still very active in the Armenian Church, but found that, beyond the music, I did not receive any spiritual nourishment for my soul. I sought out other religious practices and prayers that would strengthen my connection with God. Nine years ago, I remember declaring to God that I could not compartmentalize my life anymore. In addition to serving others, I also needed a spiritual community in which I could also receive God's love. Yet I did not know how to find it. I went through a dark night of the soul. God asked me to shake off all that stood in the way of taking that calling to another level. It was a painful shedding of skin, but in the process, I grew closer to God.

I experienced numerous losses that year: divorce, unemployment, and rejection by my Armenian Church community. No one in my church community reached out to me, and I was denied communion by a family friend.

In that same year, I married a loving man and had a beautiful child—I did not have to hide my inner spirit anymore. Even with these blessings, the journey was difficult. God asked me to let go of all the beliefs that limited me; beliefs that I am a victim because of the genocide my culture endured, beliefs that to let my spirit shine is somehow a sin. I prayed to God daily, angry at times, desolate at others. I realize that I often felt God's presence, but most of the time I was too afraid or too angry to let Him in. Losing my ability to serve as a social worker was the most painful loss of all.

When I finally let God's presence close enough so I could accept it, I could feel His radiating love, and knew that He was waiting for me to stop blaming myself. The blame and judgment I felt did not come from God. When I accepted that truth, I could let God into my heart. I asked God to take away all the pain I held onto, from the pain of my life and the pain I carried from my ancestors. Peace and unconditional love would enter my heart, and from that peaceful place, I felt the expansiveness of my soul. From that place, I knew that God's love is actually stronger than any pain we humans may inflict on ourselves or others.

So what is Christ asking of us, in this passage? To go beyond what we know and are comfortable with, to follow God. For me, part of that process includes honoring my painful experiences as part of who I am, as part of my ministry. I can't just ignore that piece and jump to the peaceful part of the story, however many times I am tempted.

Because of my life experiences, I have seen what happens when a war is considered over. People who are left behind must somehow learn to let go of survival mode and begin to learn to trust people again and to give emotionally to themselves and to their children. How people cope emotionally affects generations to come.

Because of my life experiences, I have seen what happens when some people are not valued as equal members of a village, of a country, of a church. Driving people out to walk in the desert, or driving people from a church community . . . there is little difference. The effects are devastating to someone's spirit. For that reason, I will always speak out against inequality. Even though it is at times difficult for me to do, I have come to learn that this voice of mine is also part of my calling.

Writing this sermon got me in touch with my grandmother's journey in a way I did not anticipate. I felt her losses even deeper than before. I felt the loss of all mothers who see their children suffer, and I prayed about how to heal all the mothers of my ancestors. I felt the presence of Mother Mary; she creates a space for me to enter within my heart, a place where I do not have to have words. In this space, I do not have to be linear, and I have all the room I need to let go of all the anger and fear from the stories that I have held; when we go into that place within our hearts, we can achieve wholeness again; whatever was lost or stripped from us *can* be restored. This mothering energy is not passive, but strong, protective, and giving, and we deserve to receive it. By receiving, we can begin to see our cup as full and not empty, and celebrate all that we receive and are thankful for.

I am thankful for the strength of my grandmother, for her faith in God, and for what she gave her community after walking through the desert. She was a midwife and offered healing cures for her Armenian neighbors. She continued to serve others, and in that way, she and I are connected.

I am thankful for the Armenian poet Diana Der-Hovanessian, who lovingly took me as a close friend when my Armenian church community deserted me. She taught me how to have a positive and loving connection to an Armenian.

I am thankful for Taner Akçam, a Turkish sociologist, writer, and professor of genocide studies. He has written books and given lectures acknowledging the Armenian Genocide as fact, amidst death threats and criticisms from some of his own Turkish people. He has healed many Armenians because of his willingness to speak the truth; his e-mail dialogue with me has created further healing and reconciliation within my heart.

I thank Mother Mary for opening her arms to me during prayer, showing me that my ability to nurture and love others includes my receiving her love for myself, that whatever mothering my grandmother lost when her three babies died can be restored to her and to me, in divine restoration.

I thank God for leading my family to this church, where I am nourished spiritually. Much like my grandmother, I felt I could only attend an Armenian Church, holding fast to the belief that that was the only way I could honor the identity of my people in my heart, since all else was taken away. I finally realized that I needed to be open to a new church community, to be able to sing to God and receive the spiritual nourishment that Christ offers me. I had to renounce a way of life I thought I would have led and a church community I thought I would have served. But look at all that I have received. In the renouncing, we receive so much more in return.

Appendix B

Mother's Day Sermon
by Tina Karagulian
May 9, 2010

Readings:[111]

Acts 16:9–15 NRSV
During the night Paul had a vision: there stood a man of Macedonia pleading with him and saying, *Come over to Macedonia and help us.* When he had seen the vision, we immediately tried to cross over to Macedonia, being convinced that God had called us to proclaim the good news to them. We set sail from Troas and took a straight course to Samothrace, the following day to Neapolis, and from there to Philippi , which is a leading city of the district of Macedonia and a Roman colony. We remained in this city for some days. On the Sabbath day we went outside the gate by the river, where we supposed there was a place of prayer; and we sat down and spoke to the women who had gathered there. A certain woman named Lydia, a worshiper of God, was listening to us; she was from the city of Thyatira and a dealer in purple cloth. The Lord opened her heart to listen eagerly to what was said by Paul. When she and her household were baptized, she urged us, saying, If you have judged me to be faithful to the Lord, come and stay at my home. And she prevailed upon us.

Revelation 21:10, 22–22:5 NRSV
In the spirit the angel carried me away to a great, high mountain and showed me the holy city Jerusalem coming down out of heaven from God. I saw no temple in the city, for its temple is the Lord God the Almighty and the Lamb. And the city has no need of sun or moon to shine on it, for the glory of God is its light, and its lamp is the Lamb. The nations will walk by its light, and the kings of the earth will bring their glory into it. Its gates will never be shut by day—and there will be no night there. People will bring into it the glory and the honor of the nations. But nothing unclean will enter it, nor anyone who practices

abomination or falsehood, but only those who are written in the Lamb's book of life.

Then the angel showed me the river of the water of life, bright as crystal, flowing from the throne of God and of the Lamb through the middle of the street of the city. On either side of the river is the tree of life with its twelve kinds of fruit, producing its fruit each month; and the leaves of the tree are for the healing of the nations. Nothing accursed will be found there any more. But the throne of God and of the Lamb will be in it, and his servants will worship him; they will see his face, and his name will be on their foreheads. And there will be no more night; they need no light of lamp or sun, for the Lord God will be their light, and they will reign forever and ever.

John 14:23–29 NRSV
Jesus said to Judas (not Iscariot), Those who love me will keep my word, and my Father will love them, and we will come to them and make our home with them. Whoever does not love me does not keep my words; and the word that you hear is not mine, but is from the Father who sent me.

I have said these things to you while I am still with you. But the Advocate, the Holy Spirit, whom the Father will send in my name, will teach you everything, and remind you of all that I have said to you. Peace I leave with you; my peace I give to you. I do not give to you as the world gives. Do not let your hearts be troubled, and do not let them be afraid. You heard me say to you, I am going away, and I am coming to you. If you loved me, you would rejoice that I am going to the Father, because the Father is greater than I. And now I have told you this before it occurs, so that when it does occur, you may believe.

Sermon:

Listen eagerly, invite God and Christ, be open to receiving the living and abundant waters of peace; once you are filled, then you can share what you received with others.

What is living water? Bodies of water filled with life: still waters, waters that move with a current, waters that quietly ripple . . .You know it's alive, because when you encounter it—you become alive yourself.

Take a moment and remember a body of water that comes alive for you. See yourself there. Take in some deep breaths. Breathe in the sounds and energy of that place. Remember how it refreshes and revives you. (Pause and take deep breaths.)

I've often felt expansive swimming in or standing at the edge of the ocean. In Corpus Christi, flying fish often announce themselves spontaneously where we are standing. When Walden first learned to swim in the ocean, we had to keep an eye on him because he loved jumping in the waves, far past where he could stand up. Each time we visit the ocean, his eyes just light up with life. At age nine, I was not once, but twice swallowed up by the ocean, tumbling around, not knowing if I could catch my breath—but something brought me to the surface, and it was not by human hands. But it felt like huge arms, watching my every move, restoring me to life.

For each one of us, our first body of water is the amniotic sac, in our mother's womb. That's where we were fed through a cord of nutrition, suspended and formed in living water. In the scriptures, we are told of a river, living water that God and Christ embody to make a home inside of us, claiming us. Like in the womb, we have all that we need.

I've often said that babies who remain in utero long after their due date enjoy a nice rent-free loft, Jacuzzi, and every possible amenity—why would they want to leave? In much the same way, God wants to make a home within us, to breathe inside us, to hook us up to nourishment that continually sustains us.

In Revelation, we are told that we are claimed by God, for God's name is written on our foreheads, and the temple of living water flows from God and Christ to us. I see this as a waterfall cascading down upon my head, filling me up. In Armenian, the word *jagadakeer* means destiny, or literally, what is written on the forehead. I often think of writing on the forehead as being marked and claimed by God. During our baptisms, we take the imprint of God on our foreheads, we are immersed in abundant water, and then take we take our place with our sisters and brothers of the earth, all of us claimed by God.

In Acts, we are invited to gather by a river with women who pray regularly. Imagine yourself there. Smell the fragrance of life that grows on the banks of the river. Then you notice a certain woman named Lydia . . . *a worshipper of God* . . . you notice her listening to something inside of her, and you see that her heart opened wide . . . after being baptized with water on her head, after she is fully filled by the love of God, she urges you, saying, *Come and stay at my home.* This woman, whose heart was opened and fed by God then can take action—she invites you, offering you hospitality.

Christ tells us, Those who love me will keep my word, and my Father will love them, and we will come to them and make our home with them. The Holy Spirit will also help us to remember Christ's words, and will always teach us everything we need to know. We hear, *My peace I give to you.*

Lydia shows us how: go to a place of prayer, listen eagerly, invite God and Christ, receive the living and abundant waters of peace; once filled, then share it with others.

Who is lost, motherless, abandoned, and could benefit from some of the love you have been given? Who has mothered you lately? Have you thanked that person through prayer, note, phone call, or visit? Have you thanked Mother Earth for the fruits and blessings she offers us each and every day?

I think of women who often open their homes to others: their hearts and their physical homes, too. On this Mother's Day, I think of the many mothers who formed new life within their bodies; I think of women and men who mother other people's children, nurturing life; I think of the many single parents maintaining home and family. It ain't always easy. There are days when you are spent, you have nothing left to give, and the routine of life just chugs on, keeps moving. Mothers often have it built in to their body chemistry to keep on going, almost on autopilot, and the world around us at times expects it. We can easily get lost in the rapid flow of life, and the act of sharing with others can be too much. Sometimes in loss and grief, it is hard to find your rhythm again. It takes slowing down, letting go of all that you don't need, and listening. Once again. Listening to the beat of your own heart. Listening to the Holy Spirit guiding you. Fully receiving. If you are not fully receiving, notice that.

Flight attendants often remind us to put our oxygen masks on first, before placing masks on children who are with us. It is a reminder we must constantly reapply to our lives, and we must remind and support one another in that, too. We cannot try and do it all on our own steam, or we will experience the ebb of our own energy. It is just a sign that we must receive more, that perhaps we are denying ourselves a living water that is somewhere deeper than where we are right now. So we must seek it, at all cost, paring down to what is really essential in our lives. Give to yourself first. Give yourself the oxygen. Take it in, breathe it in until your lungs are truly filled. Then give to others.

Last Sunday, we learned how to give living water to our sisters and brothers. We learned about the wonderful community project to drill for well water in places where people desperately need it. Linked to every outward action is also an inward one. There is well water also deep within each of us. There are times we need a community of loved ones to show us how to find our inner well; we may have to drill deeper to find it.

Do you give before you have had your fill of God's love? Do you say your prayers then walk away, wondering why you haven't been heard, haven't been fed? Our God who mothers us never expects for us to sacrifice what our souls need in order to serve others. Ask Her to come sit with you by the river; She remembers the moment when She created and birthed you. She knows every hair on your head, every inch of your face, and She kissed your forehead when you came to life. Ask Her and the love of Christ to enter your hearts, your inner temples, so that you may be filled. Really take a good long, swig of that love. Claim that abundance in your heart. Then any action, even what may appear to be a small step, is plenty.

Prayer is a wonderful form of action. In her book *Embraced by the Light*, Betty Eadie recounts a near-death experience where she meets Christ. She tells us

I was . . . told that there is no greater prayer than that of a mother for her children. These are the purest prayers because of their intense desire and, at time, sense of desperation. A mother has the ability to give her heart to her children and to implore mightily before God for them. She goes on to say . . . once our prayers of desire have been received, we need to let go of them and trust in the power of God to answer them . . . we must invite God's will to become our own.[112]

A similar form of action is described by Sharon Mehdi, author of *The Great Silent Grandmother Gathering.*[113] She writes

On a buffety, blustery early summer day, when the news was bad and the sky turned yellow, a strange thing happened in the town where I live.

This is the beginning of her story of two grandmothers who, by standing in the park all day long—not speaking, not looking at squirrels, not munching on coconut candy—soon have everyone in the town talking. What are they doing?

A young girl informs the stumped observers: *They're saving the world.*[113]

Two women who do something so simple that, at first, no one takes them seriously. Simple acts and words have an enormous impact on communities. When joined by other women, their simple act of caring transforms the world.

The act could also be mentoring a younger woman, teaching her to listen for the sound of her inner waterfalls, to hear the unique sound of the Holy Spirit moving in her life. Through prayer, intention, and community, great things are possible. The action of peace—the peace that Christ offers us today—can take many forms.

Jean Shinoda Bolen, author of *The Millionth Circle*, tells us that women who gather in circles to share with one another are like labyrinths:

> . . . *conversation takes a spiral shape* . . . *listening, witnessing, role modeling* . . . *deepening, mirroring, laughing* . . . *crying,* . . . *sharing of the wisdom of experience, women in circles support each other and discover themselves.*[114]

Judith Duerk, in her book *Circle of Stones*, tells us that tears, depression, and inner struggle may also be expressions of the Holy Spirit awakening a message in us. She writes:

No . . . not this way . . .
    No . . . your life has no meaning lived this way.
        No . . .
            No . . .
            Slow down.
                Rest,
                    Fill the kettle slowly.
Listen! As the water in its slender stream
        flows down to fill the waiting kettle.[115]

These are ways to mother ourselves and others. There is water inside that never runs out. This water will show you every step of your life, will guide your every action. Dig deep in your well. Find your community of mothers. Shine the light of your water with the world.

Let us pray:

Loving Mother, Christ—
Make a space within my heart
to feel your touch upon me,
your hand upon my forehead,
your signature upon my thoughts,
your words upon my lips.
Help me to sit still and wait upon you,
to earnestly move toward you,
to be filled by all that you give.
Help me to remain—
not to rush off
to take care of other things
before fully receiving you.
Steady me,
Hold me,
Fill me
with your infinite peace.
Show me how to bless
and to love myself,
so that I can share that
blessing with others.

Come—stay at my home.

Amen.

We invite all mothers and all those who mother: teachers, professors, nurses . . . all who mother; please gather around the altar during our prayers.

Prayers of the People:

Creator, Mother, we thank you for birthing us from living water, through amniotic sac and through the claiming of our divine spark. May we continue to come to you to feed on your holy water at all times, for you know our every need before we ask.

All: We bless you and honor you; open us to your wisdom, strength, and love. Come, stay in our homes and our hearts.

For all women and men who embody love and nurture in our classrooms, churches, and our communities; for adoptive parents, who claim children as their own, and for single parents who mother and father their children:

All: We bless you, and honor you; may you be filled with tender wisdom, strength, and love.

For mothers all over the world who shield and strengthen children in situations of war, poverty, and loneliness; for all who have difficulty mothering, or are in need of deep mothering—may mistakes be forgiven and your hearts, souls, and bodies be mended. For those in our community who face illness and need tender care, namely: (Fill in names).

All: May you receive blessings and strength in each moment, through those you meet each day, and through the loving embrace of God and Christ.

For all mothers, grandmothers, and foremothers of our ancestral line, those living on earth and those living in spirit, that their infinite sacrifices may be honored and acts of love remembered:

All: We bless you, and honor your immense wisdom, strength, and love.

For all mothers present here today in our sanctuary, for collectively stitching hearts together in our church community:

All: We bless you, and appreciate your tireless wisdom, strength, and love. Thank you for filling our church home.

Each mother will then pass the bowl of living water to one another, saying:

I bless you, honor you, and share God's living water with you.

After each woman is blessed, the bowl of living water is held up toward Mother Earth.

For Mother Earth, who tirelessly gives us her fruit, her shade, and her plenty—may we be ever grateful and tend to her needs, so that her presence may continue for generations:

All: We bless the fruit of your fields, ever-grateful for your love and life-giving seasons; we embrace our earthly home.

(Pause as an acolyte takes the bowl of living water to sprinkle on the ground around the labyrinth, then returns the bowl to the center of the altar.)

May we honor the vast blessings of mothers in all forms, knowing that our empty hearts will forever be filled, that through our struggles and trials we are never alone. We are open to receive, knowing that God our Mother has claimed us, and provides us with living waters to offer the world.

Amen.

Bibliography and Notes

[1]Kay Briggs, *The Magic Seashells: From a Sea of Darkness to an Ocean of Love, Healing Depression and Childhood Abuse*, (Austin: Briggs Benchmarks), 2007, 141. www.kaybriggs.com

[2]Paschal Murat Booker, *Longer Now*, (Tres Leches: SevenArtz Press), 2010. Known to many as Pat Booker, my husband is a teacher, poet, fiction writer, and in his words, *a reckless fool*. He introduced me to writing poetry when we joined our lives together, and we often write poetry under the pen name *PaTina*; we have co-authored several poetry chapbooks. Paschal has written the novels *Scarred Angels* and *Galilee*, numerous short stories, and *skillions* of poems, many of which can be found at murat11.blogspot.com.

[3]China Galland, *Longing for Darkness: Tara and the Black Madonna*, (New York: Penguin Books), 1990.

[4]Sue Monk Kidd, *The Secret Life of Bees*, (New York: Penguin Putnam, Inc.), 2002.

[5]Sue Monk Kidd, *Dance of the Dissident Daughter: A Woman's Journey from Christian Tradition to the Sacred Feminine*, (San Francisco: HarperOne), 1996.

[6]Tina Karagulian, Prayer to *Divine Mother*, 2008. After Pat and I were blessed by Divine Mother when we came together, I painted a portrait of Divine Mother as a response to that blessing. The portrait now resides at the Black Madonna Shrine of Our Lady of Czestochowa in East San Antonio. A print from the portrait and this prayer came together in the form of prayer cards to Divine Mother.

[7]Sylvia Maddox received her M.T.S. from Oblate School of Theology and teaches in the Religious Studies Department of the University of the Incarnate Word, San Antonio. She is a retreat and workshop leader on topics of prayer and spirituality, and author of *Holy Companions: Spiritual Practices from the Celtic Saints, Celtic Prayer: Recognizing God's Presence in our Every Experience*, and articles on Celtic Prayer, Saint Patrick, and Julian of Norwich; with Mary Earle, she co-authored *Praying with the Celtic Saints: Companions for the Journey*. Sylvia teaches how the rhythms of the earth are a tangible part of spirituality, as

reflected in her presentation *Celtic Spirituality: Seeing the Whole Earth as Full of God's Glory.*

[8]Carl Gustav Jung, *The Archetypes and the Collective Unconscious*, translated by R.F.C. Hull, (New York: Bollingen Series, Princeton University Press), 1959, 20–21.

[9]Jodi Roberts is a spiritual consciousness teacher and sound healer, weaving ceremony, coaching and sacred sound to catalyze growth and change. She is a cultural anthropologist trained in cross-cultural native ceremony and healing, spiritual counseling, action method psychodrama, energy healing, Zen meditation, Tibetan sound healing, and Holographic Sound Healing. She has twenty-four years of experience in mindfulness and meditation techniques for stress reduction, reality creation, energy healing, and transformational healing, and was the first sound healing/meditation specialist for the military at Ft. Hood Army Warrior Combat Stress RESET Program in Killeen, Texas. jodisacredsound@gmail.com, www.sacredinspiration.com

[10]Ona Banks Barnes is a wise spiritual leader and guide for those who seek Self-realization. She has led meditation groups and has lectured as part of the Self-Realization Fellowship, an organization led by Paramahansa Yogananda. Her strong and loving presence in the African-American community in Mississippi has been a beacon amidst a painful history of civil rights violations.

[11]Janet Morley, prayer *I Will Praise God My Beloved* in *All Desires Known: Inclusive Prayers for Worship and Meditation (Expanded Edition),* (Harrisburg: Morehouse Publishing), 1992, 91–92.

[12]Mark 5:34, *The New Oxford Annotated Bible with the Apocrypha,* Edited by Herbert G. May and Bruce M. Metzger, (New York: Oxford University Press), 1977, 1220. There are many references in the Hebrew Bible and the New Testament that outline faith's being a cooperative process with a divine figure. Other references include Matthew 9:22, Mark 3:10, Mark 5:29–34, Luke 7:50, and Luke 8:48.

[13]Carl Gustav Jung, *The Archetypes and the Collective Unconscious*, translated by R.F.C. Hull, (New York: Bollingen Series, Princeton University Press), 1959, 262.

[14]Winona Diltz describes herself as a serious student of esoteric teachings and *A Course in Miracles*, (Mill Valley: The Foundation for Inner Peace), three volumes, June 1976.

[15]Betty J. Eadie, *Embraced by the Light*, (Placerville: Gold Leaf Press and Bantam Books), 1992, 126–127. www.embracedbythelight.com

[16]Immaculée Ilibagiza, *Left to Tell: Discovering God Amidst the Rwandan Holocaust*, (with Steve Erwin), (Carlsbad: Hay House), 2006, 80. Immaculée is a voice of prayer and reconciliation in Rwanda and the world. She has written numerous books, including *Our Lady of Kibeho* and *Led by Faith: Rising from the Ashes of the Rwandan Genocide*. www.immaculee.com

[17]Ted Andrews, *Animal-Speak*, (St. Paul: Llewellyn Publications), 1996, 361.

[18]*Der Eem Asdvadz* prayer in Armenian. See footnote 20 for the translation of this prayer.

[19]Julian of Norwich, *Showings*, translated and introduced by Edmund Colledge, O.S.A. and James Walsh, S.J. (Mahwah: Paulist Press and The Missionary Society of St. Paul the Apostle in the State of New York), 1978, 295.

[20]*Der Eem Asdvadz* prayer translation by the Rev. Fr. Mikael Devejian. My mother told me that when she was a child, this prayer was taught to students of the Sahagian School in Aleppo (Halep), Syria, to be said in conjunction with the Lord's Prayer in Armenian each night.

[21]Clarissa Pinkola Estés, *Warming the Stone Child: Myths & Stories of Abandonment and the Unmothered Child, The Story of The Little Red Cap*, Audio CD, (Louisville: Sounds True), 2004. www.soundstrue.com

[22]Hans Christian Andersen, originally in Danish: *Den lille havfrue or The Little Mermaid*, (Copenhagen: C. A. Reitzel), 1837.

[23]Hayao Miyazaki, *Ponyo*, or literally *Ponyo on the Cliff*, is a 2008 Japanese animated film by Studio Ghibli, written and directed by Hayao Miyazaki. The plot centers upon a goldfish named Ponyo who befriends a five-year-old human boy, Sōsuke; Ponyo wants to become a human girl, yet on a deeper level, it shows the many parts of a woman's psyche

as it becomes integrated. Miyazaki's films satisfy the soul on a deep level, especially for women of all ages, and I have found that watching his movies more than once helps integrate the soul. Along with *Ponyo*, other Studio Ghibli productions by the director Hayao Miyazacki include *Spirited Away*, *Nausicaä of the Valley of the Wind*, and *Howl's Moving Castle*. *The Cat Returns* is directed by Hiroyuki Morita. www.ghibli.jp and www.studioghibli.net

[24]Robert A. Johnson, *Inner Work*: Using Dreams & Active Imagination for Personal Growth, (New York: HarperCollins), 1986, 28.

[25]Tina Karagulian, poem *Jagadakeer* in *Insights on the Journey: Trauma, Healing, & Wholeness, An Anthology of Women's Writing*, compiled by Maureen Leach, OSF, (San Antonio: peaceCENTER), 2008, 39.

[26]Taner Akçam, *A Shameful Act: The Armenian Genocide and the Question of Turkish Responsibility*, translated by Paula Bessemer; translation copyright by the Zoryan Institute, (New York: Metropolitan Books: Henry Holt and Company), 2006, 197–198, 202.

[27]Taner Akçam, *A Shameful Act: The Armenian Genocide and the Question of Turkish Responsibility*, translated by Paula Bessemer; translation copyright by the Zoryan Institute, (New York: Metropolitan Books: Henry Holt and Company), 2006, 278.

[28]Taner Akçam, *A Shameful Act: The Armenian Genocide and the Question of Turkish Responsibility*, translated by Paula Bessemer; translation copyright by the Zoryan Institute, (New York: Metropolitan Books: Henry Holt and Company), 2006, 278.

[29]Rev. Abraham Hartunian, *Neither to Laugh nor to Weep*, translated by Rev. Vartan Hartunian, (Cambridge: Armenian Heritage Press), 1986, 180–181.

[30]Taner Akçam, *A Shameful Act: The Armenian Genocide and the Question of Turkish Responsibility*, translated by Paula Bessemer; translation copyright by the Zoryan Institute, (New York: Metropolitan Books: Henry Holt and Company), 2006, acknowledgment page.

[31]Elaine Pagels, *The Gnostic Gospels*, (New York: Random House, later Vintage Books), 1979.

[32]Elisabeth Schüssler Fiorenza, *In Memory of Her: A Feminist Theological Reconstruction of Christian Origins*, (New York: The Crossroad Publishing Company), 1983. 229–230; 233.

[33]Medaksé, poem *It Does Not Matter* in *Anthology of Armenian Poetry*, editors Diana Der-Hovanessian and Marzbed Margossian, (New York: Columbia University Press), 1978, 331. Medaksé chooses to use only one name, and it means *made of silk*. She describes herself as a feminist and is known as the working woman's poet.

[34]Paula Jurigian, Tina Karagulian, and Sona Yeghiayan, editors. *Side by Side*. (Waltham: Self-published), Vol. 1, Issue 1, Winter 1986/1987. *Side by Side* is referenced in Barbara J. Merguerian's chapter *Oriental Orthodox Traditions and the Armenian Apostolic Church*, in *Encyclopedia of Women in Religion in North America*, Rosemary Keller Skinner, Rosemary Radford Ruether, Marie Cantlon, editors. (Bloomington: Indiana University Press), 2006, Volume 2, 521. *Side by Side* is also referenced in the commentary by Khachig Tölöyan, *The Role of the Armenian Apostolic Church in the Diaspora*, in *Armenian Review*, Vol. 41, No. 1/161, Spring 1988, 55–68. He writes: *Armenian women have been demanding a more active role in both the liturgy and the administration of church affairs since October 1968, when 51 members of the Diocese (22 women, 29 men, three of whom were clergymen) signed the* Williams Bay Manifesto. . . *Those who signed the declaration have been, in a sense, the spiritual ancestors of the group editing* Kov Kovi (Side by Side)*, which is requesting the ordination of women to the Diaconate and other reforms (Vol 1, No. 1, Winter 1986/7).* The Williams Bay Manifesto was issued at the Armenian Church Youth Organization of America (A.C.Y.O.A.) Assembly in Williams Bay, WI.

[35]Rev. Arnak Kasparian, *Memories*, (Self-published: New Jersey), 2003, 37–39, 47, 58. His article *Women, quit the choir!* was published in the *BEMA* in 1985, encouraging women to quit the choir if they were not ordained *tbir* or acolyte. This is but one of many examples of how he challenged Armenians to change church rules that were more inclusive of women.

[36]Louise Kalemkerian, *The Role of Women in the Armenian Church and Ordination to the Diaconate* presentation given at the 1986 Diocesan Assembly of the Armenian Apostolic Church, Racine, Wisconsin.

[37]Louise Kalemkerian contributed *Women in Liturgy: Why Now?* to *Side by Side*, Paula Jurigian, Tina Karagulian, and Sona Yeghiayan, editors, (Waltham: Self-published), Vol 1, Issue 1, Winter 1986/1987, 2–3. Louise Kalemkerian has co-authored, with Barbara Hovsepian, *Saints for Children: From the Tradition of the Armenian Church*, (New York: St. Vartan Press), 1983; she co-edited the *Day by Day* newsletter with Barbara Hovsepian. Her journey and writings, along with the movement toward ordination in the Armenian Apostolic Church is referenced in Barbara J. Merguerian's chapter *Oriental Orthodox Traditions and the Armenian Apostolic Church*, in *Encyclopedia of Women in Religion in North America*, Rosemary Keller Skinner, Rosemary Radford Ruether, Marie Cantlon, editors. (Bloomington: Indiana University Press), 2006, Volume 2, 518–523.

[38]Jean Shinoda Bolen, MD, *The Millionth Circle*, (York Beach: Conari Press, Red Wheel/Weiser), 1999.

[39]Barbara Hovsepian, letter to *Side by Side* editors after attending an Armenian Women's conference in Tenafly, New Jersey, 1992. Barbara Hovsepian has co-authored *Saints for Children: From the Tradition of the Armenian Church*, (New York: St. Vartan Press), 1983, and co-edited the *Day by Day* newsletter, both with Louise Kalemkerian.

[40]The Sisters of Notre Dame de Namur *"work to enable those who are materially poor to obtain what is rightfully theirs by **changing unjust structures**. We believe that education in varied forms is the best way to accomplish this goal."* Their focus is working with women and children who are poor or abandoned from all over the world. For more information, visit www.sndden.org.

[41]Sona Yeghiayan shared the following books that made a particular impact on her life: A novel of the Armenian Genocide by Micheline Aharonian Marcom, *Three Apples Fell From Heaven*, (New York: Riverhead Books), 2001; Nancy Goldberger, Jill Tarule, Blythe Clinchy, and Mary Belenky, editors, *Knowledge, Difference, and Power: Essays Inspired by Women's Ways of Knowing*, (New York: Basic Books), 1996; Mary Field Belenky, Blythe McVicker Clinchy, Nancy Rule Goldberger, and Jill Mattuck Tarule, *Women's Ways of Knowing: The Development of Self, Voice, and Mind*, (New York: Basic Books), 1986, 1997; Anne Cameron, *Annie's Poems*, (Madeira Park, BC: Harbour), 1987; and also Barbara G. Walker, *The Women's Encyclopedia of Myths and Secrets*, (San Francisco: Harper & Row), 1983.

[42]Interview with Rev. Flora A Keshgegian by Tina Karagulian, 1991; Tina Karagulian and Sona Yeghiayan, editors, *Side by Side* (Watertown: Self-published), Vol 2, Winter 1991, 2–3. Rev. Flora A. Keshgegian has authored *Redeeming Memories: A Theology of Healing and Transformation*, (Nashville: Abingdon Press), 2000, *God Reflected: Metaphors for Life*, (Minneapolis: Augsburg Fortress), 2008, *Time for Hope: Practices for Living in Today's World*, (New York: The Continuum International Publishing Group), 2006, and is referenced in Barbara J. Merguerian's chapter *Oriental Orthodox Traditions and the Armenian Apostolic Church*, in *Encyclopedia of Women in Religion in North America*, Rosemary Keller Skinner, Rosemary Radford Ruether, Marie Cantlon, editors. (Bloomington: Indiana University Press), 2006, Volume 2, 521–522. Rev. Flora Keshgegian is Associate Professor of Pastoral Theology and Women in Ministry for The Church Divinity School of the Pacific (CDSP), the Episcopal Seminary of the West. For more information, visit www.florak.org.

[43]Hagop J. Nersoyan, Ph.D., *Women and Christian Priesthood*, originally published in *Keghard*, the Armenian Youth Organization of America newsletter, 1979.

[44]Clarissa Pinkola Estés, Ph.D., *Women Who Run With the Wolves: Myths and Stories of the Wild Woman Archetype*, (New York: Ballantine Books) 1992, 49.

[45]Clarissa Pinkola Estés, Ph.D., *Women Who Run With the Wolves: Myths and Stories of the Wild Woman Archetype*, (New York: Ballantine Books) 1992, 197.

[46]Ellen Bass and Laura Davis, *The Courage to Heal: A Guide for Women Survivors of Child Sexual Abuse*, (New York: HarperCollins), 1988.

[47]Carol Sydney, *Wisdom of the Masters*, (Lincoln: Writer's Club Press), 2001, 129. Writer's Club Press is an imprint of iUniverse, www.iuniverse.com, Carol-Sydney.com

[48]Patanjali, *The Yoga Sūtras of Patanjali*, Original text, 2nd Century B.C.E; Gina Lalli taught using the translation by Rammurti S. Mishra, M.D., *Yoga Sutras, The Textbook of Yoga Psychology*, (Monroe: Baba Bhagavandas Publication Trust), www.anandaashram.org

[49]Gina Lalli, my yoga teacher who taught the sacred texts *The Yoga Sūtras of Patanjali* and *The Bhagavad Gita (The Song of the Blessed Lord)*. Gina lists the following other references: BKS Iyengar, *Light on the Yoga Sutras of Patanjali,* (Great Britain: Thorsons-HarperCollins) 1993; Swami Hariharananda Aranya, *Yoga Philosophy of Patanjali,* (Albany: State University of New York Press), 1983; Georg Feuerstein, *The Yoga-Sutra of Patanjali,* (Rochester, Vermont: Inner Traditional International), 1979; Alistair Shearer, *Effortless Being,* (London/Boston: Unwin Paperbacks), 1982. For more information on Gina Lalli's quotes and translations, please visit www.ginalalli.com/bhagavadgita.

[50]Paramahansa Yogananda, *Autobiography of a Yogi,* (Los Angeles: Self-Realization Fellowship).

[51]Yahaira Volpe, www.yahaira.org/meditation.php.

[52]From Gina Lalli's oral teaching of the Bhagavad Gita.

[53]Gina Lalli wrote about *The Bhagavad Gita (The Song of the Blessed Lord)*, which Paramahansa Yogananda describes: *This noble Sanskrit poem, which forms part of the Mahabharata epic, is the Hindu Bible.* Paramahansa Yogananda, *Autobiography of a Yogi,* (Los Angeles: Self-Realization Fellowship), 1946, 6. Gina Lalli recommends Eliot Deutsch's translation of *The Bhagavad Gita,* (Holt, Rinehart & Winston), 1968, or Eknath Easwaran's translation, The Blue Mountain Center of Meditation, (Tomales: Nilgiri Press), 1985, www.nilgiri.org. For more information on Gina Lalli's translation, visit www.ginalalli.com/bhagavadgita

[54]Paramahansa Yogananda, *Autobiography of a Yogi,* (Los Angeles: Self-Realization Fellowship).

[55]Gina Lalli, wrote about yoga on her website, based on her study of *The Yoga Sūtras of Patanjali* and *The Bahavad Gita (The Song of the Blessed Lord)*, www.ginalalli.com/bhagavadgita

[56]Paramahansa Yogananda, *Autobiography of a Yogi,* (Los Angeles: Self-Realization Fellowship).

[57]Sandra Ingerman, *Soul Retrieval: Mending the Fragmented Self* (Harper San Francisco), 1991. www.sandraingerman.com

[58]Tina Karagulian, *The Annunciation of My Soul*, in *Lifting Women's Voices: Prayers to Change the World*, Margaret Rose, Jenny Te Paa, Jeanne Person, and Abagail Nelson, editors, (New York: Morehouse Publishing), 2009, 171. The author's version of prayer printed in this publication.

[59]Clarissa Pinkola Estés, Ph.D., *Women Who Run With the Wolves: Myths and Stories of the Wild Woman Archetype*, (New York: Ballantine Books) 1992, 128–129.

[60]John 16:24, *The New Oxford Annotated Bible with the Apocrypha*, Edited by Herbert G. May and Bruce M. Metzger, (New York: Oxford University Press), 1977, 1311. There are many Bible references that demonstrate the many times that we ask, we will be given what we need. Some references include Matthew 7:7, Matthew 21:22, Luke 11:9, and John 14:13–14, pages 1179, 1199, 1261, and 1309 respectively.

[61]Dr. Luke Timothy Johnson shared his personal story during the presentation *Scripture & Discernment: Decision-Making and the Living God* through the Work+Shop and St. Mark's Episcopal Church, San Antonio, Texas, January 8–10, 2010. Dr. Luke Timothy Johnson is the Robert W. Woodruff Professor of New Testament and Christian Origins at Emory University's Candler School of Theology in Atlanta, Georgia. A former Benedictine monk, Professor Johnson is the author of more than 20 books, including *The Real Jesus: The Misguided Quest for the Historical Jesus and the Truth of the Traditional Gospels* and *The Writings of the New Testament: An Interpretation*. For more information, visit www.candler.emory.edu and www.theworkshop-sa.org.

[62]Diana Der-Hovanessian, New England-born poet, was twice a Fulbright professor of American Poetry and is the author of more than 23 books of poetry and translations. Her poems have appeared in *Agni, American Poetry Review, Ararat, CSM, Poetry, Partisan, Prairie Schooner, Nation*, and in anthologies such as *Against Forgetting, Women on War, On Prejudice, Finding Home, Leading Contemporary Poets, Orpheus and Company, Identity Lessons, Voices of Conscience,* and *Two Worlds Walking*. Two of her plays, *The Secret of Survival* and *Growing Up Armenian*, were produced and in 1984 and 1985, and traveled to many college campuses in the 1980s, telling the Armenian story with poetry and music. After 1989, *The Secret of Survival*, with Michael

Kermoyan and later with Vahan Khanzadian, was performed for earthquake relief benefits. Diana works as a visiting poet and guest lecturer on American poetry, Armenian poetry in translation, and the literature of human rights, at various universities here and abroad. She serves as president of the New England Poetry Club. Her books of poetry include *The Second Question, The Burning Glass, Any Day Now, About Time, How to Choose Your Past,* and *Songs of Bread, Songs of Salt.* Her Armenian to English translations include *The Other Voice: Armenian Women's Poetry, Anthology of Armenian Poetry,* and *The Armenian Prayerbook of St. Gregory of Narek* with Thomas J. Samuelian (Yerevan: Vem Press), 2002. St. Gregory of Narek (951–1003) wrote his mystical prayers in *Girk' aghot' its* or *Book of Prayer,* also known as the *Book of Lamentations.* Her book *Selected Poems* was nominated for the Pulitzer Prize. Her latest book of poetry is *Dancing at the Monastery* through Sheep Meadow Press, 2011. www.dianaderhovanessian.com

[63]Mary C. Earle, *Beginning Again: Benedictine Wisdom for Living with Illness,* (New York: Morehouse Publishing), 2004, 49. Mary Earle is an Episcopal priest, spiritual director, retreat leader and author of *The Desert Mothers: Spiritual Practices from the Women of the Wilderness.* Author of four books and co-author of two, Mary is also a published poet. Her ministry focuses on spiritual direction, contemplative prayer and interfaith dialogue. She is an adjunct faculty member of the Seminary of the Southwest in Austin, and Author in Residence at The Work+Shop, a ministry of St. Mark's Episcopal Church in San Antonio, Texas. She is also the co-contributor to the audio CD set of *Telling the Brothers: Perspectives on Mary Magdalene: A conversation with Reverend Mary Earle and Reverend Jane Patterson.* Her latest book is entitled *Celtic Christian Spirituality: Essential Writings—Annotated and Explained*; Foreword by John Philip Newell. www.maryearle.org www.churchpublishing.org

[64]Henry David Thoreau, *Walden* or *Life in the Woods and On the Duty of Civil Disobedience,* (New York: The New American Library of World Literature, Inc.) 1960, 215.

[65]Barsegh Kanachyan or Parsegh Ganachyan, (1885–1967), composed an arrangement of the traditional Armenian lullaby *Oror Im Balas* or *Օրոր Իմ Բալաս.*

[66]Margaret Ajemian Ahnert, *The Knock at the Door: A Journey Through the Darkness of the Armenian Genocide*, (New York: Beaufort Books), 2007, 108. www.margaretahnert.com

[67]Clarissa Pinkola Estés, Ph.D., from an interview on Sounds True, www.soundstrue.com/articles/A_Life_Made_by_Hand_with_Clarissa_Pinkola_Estes/

[68]Carol S. Pearson, Ph.D., *Awakening the Heroes Within: Twelve Archetypes to Help us Find Ourselves and Transform our World*, (New York: HarperCollins), 1991, 161.

[69]Tina Karagulian, prayer *My Heart is Full* in *Sustaining Abundant Life*, (San Antonio: The Episcopal Diocese of West Texas Education Department), 2009, 21. The prayer was inspired by the poetry and art of Martha K. Grant. The book supports *Woman at the Well House: Leading Women to a New Way of Life, Hope, & Faith.* www.womenatthewellhouse.org; Ruth 3:11, *The New Oxford Annotated Bible with the Apocrypha*, Edited by Herbert G. May and Bruce M. Metzger, (New York: Oxford University Press), 1977, 328.

[70]Tina Karagulian delivered this sermon about her grandmother's journey through the desert during the Armenian Genocide, linking it with our own spiritual times in the desert, The Episcopal Church of Reconciliation, San Antonio, Texas, September 9, 2007. See Appendix A.

[71]Makar Yekmalian, *Soorp, Soorp (Holy, Holy)* hymn, in the *Sacred Music of the Armenian Church, Volume II,* by Vartan Sarxian, arr. Socrates Boyajian, (New York: Eastern Diocese of the Armenian Church of America), 1993, 1920.

[72]Taner Akçam, Ph.D. author of *A Shameful Act: The Armenian Genocide and the Question of Turkish Responsibility,* (New York: Henry Holt and Company), 2006, and guest lecturer on Reconciliation for Armenian and Turkish communities. Associate Professor, Department of History, Robert Aram and Marianne Kaloosdian and Stephen and Marion Mugar Chair, The Strassler Family Center for Holocaust and Genocide Studies, Clark University, Worcester, MA. www.clarku.edu

[73]Dawna Markova, *I Will Not Die an Unlived Life: Reclaiming Purpose and Passion*, (San Francisco: Conari Press, Red Wheel/Weiser), 2000, 127.

[74]*The Secret of Kells*, story by Tomm Moore, directed by Tomm Moore and Nora Twomey, screenplay by Fabrice Ziolkowski, 2009. Young Brendan lives in a remote medieval monastery under siege from barbarian raids. When a celebrated master illuminator arrives from foreign lands carrying an ancient but unfinished book, his creativity is piqued. To help complete the magical book, Brendan has to overcome his deepest fears on a dangerous quest that takes him into the enchanted forest where mythical creatures hide. It is here that he meets the fairy Aisling, a mysterious young wolf-girl, who helps him find his way. www.cartoonsaloon.ie www.kellsmovie.com

[75]The Christ Healing Center offers *Theophostic Prayer Ministry* as a means to bring about Christ's healing. Theophostic prayer encourages individuals to have a direct experience and interaction with Christ. www.theophostic.com, www.christhealingcenter.org

[76]Tsultrim Allione, *Feeding Your Demons: Ancient Wisdom for Resolving Inner Conflict*, (New York: Little Brown and Company), 2008, 257–260. This book connects the knowledge of Tibetan Buddhism with the modern psyche, addressing major cultural issues and the roots of our suffering. This national bestseller is based on Lama Tsultrim's pioneering technique, using five steps to nurture the parts of ourselves we usually fight. Her teachings focus on the lineage of Machig Labdrön, the 11th century Tibetan yogini who founded the Chöd lineage. Inspired by the vision of a Western retreat center, while living in the Himalayas in the 1970s, Lama Tsultrim founded Tara Mandala with her husband David Petit in 1994, where she is now the spiritual director and resident teacher. Lama Tsultrim was one of the first American women to be ordained as a Tibetan nun in 1970 by the 16th Karmapa. At the age of 26, after four years as a nun, she returned her monastic vows, married, and raised a family of three. Lama Tsultrim earned a master's degree in Buddhist Studies and Women's Studies from Antioch University. She is the author of *Women of Wisdom*, a groundbreaking book on the lives of great female Tibetan practitioners. More about the life and teachings of Machig Labdrön is written in *Women of Wisdom*, (Boston: Routledgte and Kegan Paul in 1984, later Ithaca: Snow Lion Publications), 2000. www.taramandala.org

[77]Rev. Jack Sheffield, *God's Healing River,* (Austin: Morgan Printing), 2003, 171.

[78]Tina Karagulian delivered this Mother's Day sermon at The Episcopal Church of Reconciliation, San Antonio, Texas, May 9, 2010. *Listen eagerly, invite God and Christ, be open to receiving the living and abundant waters of peace; once you are filled, then you can share what you received with others.* Acts 16:9–15; Revelation 21:10, 22–22:5; John 14:23–29. See Appendix B.

[79]Matthew 22:37–39, *The New Oxford Annotated Bible with the Apocrypha*, Edited by Herbert G. May and Bruce M. Metzger, (New York: Oxford University Press), 1977, 1201. References in the Hebrew Bible include Leviticus 19:18 and Deuteronomy 6:5, pages 146, 223.

[80]Romans 8:28, *New Revised Standard Version Bible*, (New York: The Division of Christian Education of the National Council of the Churches of Christ), 1989, 1921.

[81]Genesis 1:27, *The New Oxford Annotated Bible with the Apocrypha*, Edited by Herbert G. May and Bruce M. Metzger, (New York: Oxford University Press), 1977, 2.

[82]John 10:30, *The New Oxford Annotated Bible with the Apocrypha*, Edited by Herbert G. May and Bruce M. Metzger, (New York: Oxford University Press), 1977, 1303. *I and my Father are One.* I see this quote as an invitation to become one with our God, no matter our name for our Creator. For me that has been God as Mother.

[83]Diana Der-Hovanessian, poem *Teaching a Child to Dance* in *The Circle Dancers*, (New York: Sheep Meadow Press), 1996, 13. This book was winner of the Paterson Prize.

[84]Clarissa Pinkola Estés, Ph.D., *The Faithful Gardener: A Wise Tale about That Which Can Never Die,* (New York: HarperCollins), 1995, 23.

[85]Clarissa Pinkola Estés, Ph.D., *The Faithful Gardener: A Wise Tale about that which can never Die,* (New York: HarperCollins), 1995, 35.

[86]MarcyCalhoun, *Are You Really Too Sensitive?* (Marysville: Intuitive Development Publishing), 1987, 85. www.marcycalhoun.com

[87]Carol Edgarian, *Rise the Euphrates*, (New York: Random House), 1994, 40. www.caroledgarian.com

[88]Carol Edgarian, *Rise the Euphrates*, (New York: Random House), 1994, 42. www.caroledgarian.com

[89]Margaret Ajemian Ahnert, *The Knock at the Door: A Journey Through the Darkness of the Armenian Genocide*, (New York: Beaufort Books), 2007, xx. www.margaretahnert.com

[90]Carol Edgarian, *Rise the Euphrates*, (New York: Random House), 1994, 6. www.caroledgarian.com

[91]D. Phelps, *Making Room for George: A Love Story,* (Bloomington: Balboa Press, a division of Hay House), 2013, 97.

[92]Barbara G. Walker, *The Women's Encyclopedia of Myths and Secrets*, (San Francisco: Harper & Row), 1983, 490.

[93]Sue Monk Kidd, *Dance of the Dissident Daughter: A Woman's Journey from Christian Tradition to the Sacred Feminine*, (San Francisco: HarperOne), 1996, 186.

[94]Sue Monk Kidd, *Dance of the Dissident Daughter: A Woman's Journey from Christian Tradition to the Sacred Feminine*, (San Francisco: HarperOne), 1996, 186.

[95]Sue Monk Kidd, *Dance of the Dissident Daughter: A Woman's Journey from Christian Tradition to the Sacred Feminine*, (San Francisco: HarperOne), 1996, 187.

[96]Robert Walden, from his class on spiritual direction as part of *The Center for Spiritual Growth and the Contemplative Life*, an organization founded by Deborah Hanus. Deborah Hanus and Robert Walden co-teach spiritual direction as part of an ecumenical community in San Antonio, Texas. Spiritual directors are companions who are committed to listening and responding to the spiritual hungers of our times by nurturing spiritual renewal and growth, and by cultivating a contemplative stance toward life. Robert Walden is also a former Catholic priest; a portion of his story of leaving the priesthood, along with other Catholic priests, appears in a book entitled *Shattered Vows: Priests Who Leave* by David Rice, (New York: William Morrow & Company, Inc.), 1990.

[97]Olga Samples Davis, *Things My Mama Told Me: The Wisdom That Shapes Our Lives*, (Colorado Springs: WaterBrook Press, a division of Random House), 2004, 116–117.

[98]Henry David Thoreau, *Walden* or *Life in the Woods and On the Duty of Civil Disobedience*, (New York: The New American Library of World Literature, Inc.) 1960, 215.

[99]Rosalyn Falcon Collier is co-founder of the San Antonio peaceCENTER (founded in 1995); she has also been a founding member of the Women on Pilgrimage Retreat at St Anthony de Padua since 1997. A native of San Antonio, she is a 1990 graduate of the Shalem Institute for Spiritual Formation in Washington, DC, and has led local meditation groups in Catholic parishes since 1997. Rosalyn recently co-facilitated the *Called Back to the Well Spiritual Renewal Program* (2009). She is a spiritual director and mediator and facilitates skillshops on nonviolence and transformative mediation. She is one of the spiritual conveners for the Ecumenical Contemplative Week: People of Pilgrimage at Oblate School of Theology. Her writings include *Peace Is Our Birthright: The P.E.A.C.E. Process And Interfaith Community Development, Walking Jesus' Path of Peace, Shall We Ever Rise?: A Holy Walk, Working It Out!: Managing And Mediating Everyday Conflicts,* and *Forgive and Remember: 33 Classic Stories About Forgiveness.* www.salsa.net/peace/peace

[100]Jean Springer, Spiritual Director as *Amma* or *Mother*. Eremos (*eh-ray-mos*) is the Greek word meaning solitary place, quiet place, desert place. Jean Springer arrived in Austin, Texas with a dream of providing a space in which people could be invited to listen to the Spirit dwelling within each of them and within the lives they live. Eremos provides spiritual support groups, prayer reflections, prayer requests, and spiritual direction. www.eremos.org

[101]The original location of this Mahatma Gandhi's quote is unknown, per consultation with his grandson Arun Gandhi. Mahatma Gandhi's autobiography was very influential in my spiritual formation. He was a pioneer of satyagaha—resistance through mass civil disobedience strongly founded on *ahimsa* (total non-violence). Mohandas Karamchand Gandhi, *Gandhi An Autobiography: The Story of My Experiments With Truth*, translated by Mahadev H. Desai, (Boston: Beacon Press and the Navajivan Trust), 1957. www.navajivantrust.org

[102]Betty J. Eadie, *Embraced by the Light*, (Placerville: Gold Leaf Press and Bantam Books), 1992, 65. www.embracedbythelight.com

[103]Elizabeth Gilbert, *Eat, Pray, Love: One Woman's Search for Everything Across Italy, India, and Indonesia*, (New York: Viking Penguin, then Penguin Books), 2006, 260.

[104]Clarissa Pinkola Estés, Ph.D., from an interview on Sounds True, www.soundstrue.com/articles/A_Life_Made_by_Hand_with_Clarissa_Pi nkola_Estes/

[105]Ted Andrews, *Animal-Speak*, (St. Paul: Llewellyn Publications), 1996, x.

[106]Ted Andrews, *Animal-Speak*, (St. Paul: Llewellyn Publications), 1996, 200–205.

[107]Ted Andrews, *Animal-Speak*, (St. Paul: Llewellyn Publications), 1996, 322–323.

[108]D. Phelps, *Making Room for George: A Love Story*, (Bloomington: Balboa Press, a division of Hay House), 2013, 205.

[109]Tina Karagulian and Zarman Meguerditchian, *It Is Time*, a co-created Reconciliation prayer.

[110]Luke 14:33, from Gospel reading Luke 14:25–33, *The New Oxford Annotated Bible with the Apocrypha*, Edited by Herbert G. May and Bruce M. Metzger, (New York: Oxford University Press), 1977, 1268.

[111]*New Revised Standard Version Bible*, (New York: The Division of Christian Education of the National Council of the Churches of Christ), 1989; 1886, 2112–2113, 1843.

[112]Betty J. Eadie, *Embraced by the Light*, (Placerville: Gold Leaf Press and Bantam Books), 1992, 104. www.embracedbythelight.com

[113]Sharon Mehdi, *The Great Silent Grandmother Gathering: A Story for Anyone Who Thinks She Can't Save the World*, (New York: Viking Penguin Group), 2004, 14.

[114]Jean Shinoda Bolen, MD, *The Millionth Circle*, (York Beach: Conari Press, Red Wheel/Weiser), 1999, 14.

[115]Judith Duerk, *Circle of Stones*, (Makawao, Maui: Inner Ocean Publishing, Inc., originally published by Innis Free Press, Inc.), 1989, 60.

Permissions

1. Ted Andrews, *Animal Speak: The Spiritual & Magical Powers of Creatures Great and Small* by Ted Andrews © 2002 Llewellyn Worldwide, Ltd. 2143 Wooddale Drive, Woodbury, MN 55125. All rights reserved, used by permission and with the best wishes of the publisher. This permission is nonexclusive and limited to the use specified here, both print and electronic uses. Permission must be requested for editions in languages other than English.

2. Immaculée Ilibagiza, *Left to Tell: Discovering God Amidst the Rwandan Holocaust,* (with Steve Erwin), (Carlsbad, CA: Hay House, Inc.), Copyright ©2006. Permission granted by the publisher and David Steffen of Isaro Consulting—a division of Immaculée Ilibagiza LLC.

3. Excerpts from Carol Edgarian, *Rise the Euphrates,* (New York: Random House), Copyright ©1994. Reprinted with permission of the author, who retains sole copyright. www.caroledgarian.com

4. Olga Samples Davis, *Things My Mama Told Me: The Wisdom That Shapes Our Lives,* (Colorado Springs: WaterBrook Press, a division of Random House), Copyright ©2004. Reprinted with permission of the author, who retains sole copyright.

5. Diana Der-Hovanessian, poem *Teaching a Child to Dance* in *The Circle Dancers*, (New York: Sheep Meadow Press), Copyright ©1996. Permission to reprint poem granted by the author, who retains sole copyright.

6. Medaksé, poem *It Does Not Matter* in *Anthology of Armenian Poetry*, translated by Diana Der-Hovanessian, editors Diana Der-Hovanessian and Marzbed Margossian, (New York: Columbia University Press). Permission to reprint poem granted by the author, who retains sole copyright.

7. Marcy Calhoun, *Are You Really Too Sensitive?* (Marysville: Intuitive Development Publishing), Copyright ©1987. Permission to reprint quote granted by the author. www.marcycalhoun.com

8. Quotes from *The Knock at the Door*, copyright ©2007 by Margaret Ajemian Ahnert, used with permission from Beaufort Books.

9. Permission granted from Yahaira Volpe to reprint information from her website www.yahaira.org/meditation.php

10. Permission granted from Gina Lalli to reprint quotes from her website www.ginalalli.com.

11. Quotes from D. Ellis Phelps, *Making Room for George: A Love Story*, (Bloomington: Balboa Press, a division of Hay House) Copyright © 2013, www.balboapress.com. Reprinted with permission from author.

12. Permission granted to use excerpt from *Autobiography of a Yogi* by Paramahansa Yogananda through Self-Realization Fellowship, Los Angeles, CA.

13. Permission to reprint quote by Mahatma Gandhi granted from his grandson Arun Gandhi.

14. Quote from Mary C. Earle, *Beginning Again: Benedictine Wisdom for Living with Illness*, (New York: Morehouse Publishing), Copyright © 2004. Reprinted with permission from author.

15. Janet Morley, *All Desires Known: Inclusive Prayers for Worship and Meditation (Expanded Edition),* (Harrisburg: Morehouse Publishing), Copyright ©1992. Excerpts from the prayer *I Will Praise God My Beloved* reprinted with permission.

16. Permission granted by Rev. Flora A. Keshgegian to reprint excerpt of 1991 *Side by Side* interview; Interview with Rev. Flora A Keshgegian by Tina Karagulian, 1991; Tina Karagulian and Sona Yeghiayan, editors, *Side by Side* (Watertown: Self-published), Vol. 2, Copyright ©1991.

17. Permission granted by author Louise Kalemkerian to reprint excerpt of article *Women in Liturgy: Why Now?* from *Side by Side*, Paula Jurigian, Tina Karagulian, and Sona Yeghiayan, editors, (Waltham: Self-published), Vol. 1, Issue 1, Copyright ©1986/1987.

18. Permission to reprint quote from her letter to the editors of *Side by Side* granted by Barbara Hovsepian.

19. Permission to reprint quote granted by Rosalyn Falcon Collier.

30. Rev. Abraham Hartunian, *Neither to Laugh nor to Weep*, (Cambridge: Armenian Heritage Press), Copyright ©1986. Permission to reprint granted by the Hartunian family.

31. Hagop J. Nersoyan, Ph.D., *Women and Christian Priesthood* in *Keghard*, the Armenian Youth Organization of America newsletter, Copyright ©1979. Full permission granted to use the article, as published, by the Armenian Youth Organization of America.

32. Excerpt from Dawna Markova, *I Will Not Die an Unlived Life: Reclaiming Purpose and Passion*, (San Francisco: Conari Press, Red Wheel/Weiser), Copyright ©2000 by Dawna Markova. Permission to reprint granted by publisher. www.redwheelweiser.com, 1-800-423-7087.

33. Excerpts from *The Millionth Circle*, (York Beach: Conari Press, Red Wheel/Weiser), Copyright ©1999 by Jean Shinoda Bolen, MD. Permission to reprint granted by publisher. www.redwheelweiser.com, 1-800-423-7087.

34. Henry David Thoreau, *Walden* or *Life in the Woods and On the Duty of Civil Disobedience*, (New York: The New American Library of World Literature, Inc.) 1960. Quotes by Henry David Thoreau are public domain.

35. Scripture texts on pages 1843, 1886, 1921, 2112, 2113 are from the *New Revised Standard Version of the Bible*, Copyright ©1989 by the Division of Christian Education of the National Council of the Churches of Christ in the USA. All rights reserved.

36. *The Secret of Kells*, story by Tomm Moore, directed by Tomm Moore and Nora Twomey, screenplay by Fabrice Ziolkowski, Copyright © 2009. Tomm Moore grants full permission to reference the story of *The Secret of Kells*. www.cartoonsaloon.ie

37. The office of Gloria Steinem grants full permission to reprint her quote.

38. Carol Sydney, author of *Wisdom of the Masters*, grants full permission to use individual quotes from conversation as well as reprint an excerpt from *Wisdom of the Masters*, Copyright ©2001.

39. Tsultrim Allione, Tara Mandala Meditation Center, and Little, Brown and Company grant permission to reference *Feeding Your Demons: Ancient Wisdom for Resolving Inner Conflict*, Copyright ©2008.

40. Rev. Jack Sheffield, *God's Healing River,* (Austin: Morgan Printing), Copyright ©2003. Reprinted with permission from the author.

41. Scripture quotations on pages 2, 146, 223, 328, 1201, 1220, 1268, 1303, 1311, are from *Revised Standard Version of the Bible, Apocrypha*, Copyright © 1957; The Third and Fourth Books of the Maccabees and Psalm 151, Copyright © 1977 National Council of the Churches of Christ in the United States of America. Used by permission. All rights reserved.

42. Quote from Elizabeth Gilbert, *Eat, Pray, Love: One Woman's Search for Everything Across Italy, India, and Indonesia,* (New York: Viking Penguin, then Penguin Books), Copyright ©2006. Permission to reprint granted by publisher.

43. Sharon Mehdi, *The Great Silent Grandmother Gathering: A Story for Anyone Who Thinks She Can't Save the World*, (New York: Viking Penguin Group), Copyright ©2004. Permission granted by publisher.

44. Kay Briggs, *The Magic Seashells: From a Sea of Darkness to an Ocean of Love, Healing Depression and Childhood Abuse*, (Austin: Briggs Benchmarks), Copyright ©2007. Author grants full permission to reprint excerpt.

45. Permission to print verbal quotes and/or stories granted by Ona Banks Barnes, Walden Booker, Rosalyn Falcon Collier, Erma Crumedy, Winona Diltz, Dru Dunn, Michelli Gomez, Eleanor Johnson, Dr. Luke Timothy Johnson, Paula Jurigian, Ardis Karagulian, Noubar Karagulian, Siran Karagulian, Rev. Arnak Kasparian, Sylvia Maddox, Yeretzkin Yefkin Megherian, Narjis Pierre, Robert Walden, and Sona Yeghiayan.

www.ingramcontent.com/pod-product-compliance
Lightning Source LLC
Chambersburg PA
CBHW072114270326
41931CB00010B/1560